The old-time pamphlet ethos is back, with some of the most challenging work being done today. Prickly Paradigm Press is devoted to giving serious authors free rein to say what's right and what's wrong about their disciplines and about the world, including what's never been said before. The result is intellectuals unbound, writing unconstrained and creative texts about meaningful matters.

"Long live Prickly Paradigm Press.... Long may its flaming pamphlets lift us from our complacency."
—Ian Hacking

Prickly Paradigm is marketed and distributed by The University of Chicago Press.

www.press.uchicago.edu

A list of current and future titles can be found on our website and at the back of this pamphlet.

www.prickly-paradigm.com

Executive Publisher
Marshall Sahlins

Publishers
Peter Sahlins
Ramona Naddaff
Seminary Co-op Bookstore

Editor
Matthew Engelke
info@prickly-paradigm.com

Design and layout by Daniel Murphy.

T0083840

Kinds of Value

Kinds of Value:
An Experiment in Modal Anthropology

Paul Kockelman

PRICKLY PARADIGM PRESS
CHICAGO

Prickly Paradigm Press, LLC
5629 South University Avenue
Chicago, IL 60637

www.prickly-paradigm.com

ISBN: 9780996635585
LCCN: 2020941170

Printed in the United States of America on acid-free paper.

Contents

1. Nuts to an Anthropological Theory of Value

Let me begin by summarizing a story, originally told by a speaker of the Mayan language Q'eqchi': "There was a man who was blind. Having heard that the god Chajul produced many miracles, he went to visit him. When he arrived at the temple, he asked that his eyes be healed, and gave a gold chain as an offering. On his way out, just as he was leaving the temple, he saw that his eyes could see (pun in the original). Great was the joy in the man's heart that his eyes were now open. Returning home, he said, 'It's a shame that I gave my gold chain. It is very expensive. I could have left a very cheap offering and my eyes would probably still have been opened.' Having said this, the man felt something heavy in his pocket. When he reached inside, he discovered that it was the gold chain. Immediately he became blind again. Realizing that he had done something wrong (*ink'a' us*, or "not good"), he said inside his heart, 'Why did I say that the chain was very expensive in comparison to [literally "in the eyes of"] my eyes?' There it dawned on the man that he had not given the offering with all his heart."

While the story ends there, the storyteller continues: "Well, that is an example for us as well. What we give, what we offer, we give with all our heart. Because if we do not give with all our heart, then neither will God [*Dios*] accept what we offer."

As a morality tale, or a brief essay on ethics, this story should be relatively recognizable (and not particularly remarkable). Having made an expensive offering to a god and received a priceless gift in return, a man regrets having offered so much (when less might have done just as well). Not having given with all his heart, and commensurating the incommensurable along the way, the man has his offering returned and the gift is taken away. Finding himself blind again, the man has gained insight as to how one should conduct oneself in life. Finally, as seen in the metacommentary at the end, this portrayal of the good, through the exchange of goods, is easily ported from the world so narrated (involving the man, the god Chajul, and the relative worth of gold chains and sighted eyes) to the world of narration (involving "us," "God," and exchange more generally).

In what follows I'm going to take up various aspects of this story, and its telling, to lay out some key features of value—both value in relation to language and value more generally. While value is, to be sure, a slippery concept, it might be initially captured with a casual gloss, as that which lies at the intersection of what agents (such as the man) strive for and what signs (such as the story) stand for. For example, gold, sight, giving with all one's heart, the good life, and even godliness itself. From this vantage, there are many different ways of framing value. My goal in this essay is not to promote any particular frame (and thereby argue that one framing of value is more valuable than others, or the most valuable of all), but rather to highlight some of the key features of some important and pervasive frames, insofar as they are figured by speakers of Q'eqchi'. As will be seen, value—as that which lies at the intersection of meaning and motivation, or that which stands at the interface of significance and selection—is not just the core topic of anthropology (indeed, it is all that anthropologists have ever studied), it is the ultimate concern of any life-form or form of life (when suitably framed).

As will become apparent, most of the evaluative frames in question turn on *relations between relations*. And, very roughly speaking, whereas the earlier sections will tend to foreground meaning, infrastructure, and means, the latter sections will tend to foreground motivation, imaginaries, and ends. The overarching goal of this essay, then, is to interrelate some of these relations between relations, qua evaluative frames, not so much by theorizing them (indeed, there is an enormous literature on each and every one of them), but rather by deploying them. In particular, by deploying them in a small work of interpretation, one that seeks to make an offering of another kind: a Mayan theory of value. Along the way, to be sure, I will foreground some of my own values: concerning, specifically, the methods one should use, the efforts one should go to, and the effects one should strive for—as an anthropologist (linguist, critical theorist, historian, economist, psychologist, philosopher, or cognitive scientist; for the topic itself is important, not some discipline's attempt to enclose it)—to produce a valuable interpretation or a worthwhile intervention. Phrased another way, meaning and motivation, significance and selection, standing for and striving for, have no disciplinary home: to study them you can (and must) go almost anywhere.

Insofar as I will be constantly moving across frames, rather than sticking to any particular frame, and insofar as many of the core ideas relate to modality, qua possible worlds, or worlding and worldliness per se, this essay might be best subtitled an exercise of, or experiment in, modal anthropology.

2. A Relation between Agents Mediated by a Relation between Entities

Across a wide variety of key texts in (what should be) the anthropological canon, value is understood as a relation between relations. In the *Nicomachean Ethics*, for example, Aristotle argued that distributive justice turns on ratios. As your (social) status is to my status, so should your share (of some common good) be relative to my share. For example, if I am a knight and you are a knave, then I should receive ten chickens from the king and you should receive two (see figure 1). Marx offered a related logic in *Capital*: value is a relation between people (say, factory owners and workers) mediated by a relation between things (say, means of production and labor power) (see figure 2). And E. E. Evans-Pritchard explicitly argued that relations between relations were at the heart of the ethnographic project. Recall, for example, his discussion of bridewealth among the Nuer, and their proportional distribution of cattle to various maternal and paternal kin.

$$\frac{\text{Share \#1}}{\text{Status \#1}} = \frac{\text{Share \#2}}{\text{Status \#2}}$$

Figure 1. Shares in Relation to Statuses (Aristotle)

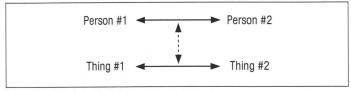

Figure 2. People in Relation to Things (Marx)

6

Such a logic is readily generalized: *value is a relation between agents mediated by a relation between entities,* where the agents need not be people and the entities need not be things. For example, the relation between students and teachers is mediated, in part, by the relation between questions and answers. And the relation between animals and plants is mediated, in part, by the relation between carbon dioxide and oxygen. Crucially, in a line of thinking most forcibly articulated by Marx, any agent is itself constituted by the ensemble of relations (between relations) it is implicated in. So far as such relations shift and transform, so does the power or identity of the agent in question. Note how portable such a vision of value is.

The story that opens this book seems to voice a similar logic several times over. A relation between exchanged entities (seeing eyes and golden chains) mediates a relation between exchanging agents (a blind man and the god Chajul). Moreover, the relation between the narrated world and the world of narration (as "entities") mediates the relation between the denizens of the former and the denizens of the latter (as "agents") (see figure 3). Phrased another way, and looking slightly ahead, a semiotic relation between

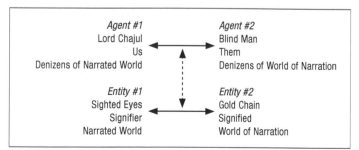

Figure 3. A Relation between Agents Mediated by a Relation between Entities

signifier and signified (or sign and object), mediates a social relation between those who signify ("us") and those who are signified ("them").

The story is, to be sure, a long way off from Aristotle's original vision of distributive justice, which presumed an equality of ratios, and hence the relative commensurability of statuses and the relative commensurability of shares. In particular, just as the agents are relatively incommensurate (a god's status, or power, cannot really be compared with a man's), so are the entities in question (the value of sight cannot—or at least *should* not—be compared with the price of gold). Moreover, the core issue is not the equivalence of the return, but rather the sincerity or selflessness of the offer. Such an infinite being will swap (priceless) sight for (expensive) gold, or even the same faculty for a cheaper offering, so long as the one making the offering does so without misgivings or machinations.

Indeed, such facts are, in some sense, the whole point of the story. So it should be remembered that this story by a nameless narrator, like Aristotle's *Nicomachean Ethics*, Marx's *Capital*, and Evans-Pritchard's *Kinship and Marriage among the Nuer*, is yet another way of framing value. While perhaps not as valuable a framing of value (in the general scheme of Western culture); it is infinitely more valuable if one wants to understand something about (a short strand in, or brief moment of) Q'eqchi'-Maya culture.

3. Saussurean Values

We just saw how the relation between agents is mediated by a relation between entities. We now focus on one way of mediating the relation between entities. From Ferdinand de Saussure, we learn that the value (or identity) of a sign is constituted by its relation to all the other signs (in some language or system) that can combine with it (to make up a composite sign) or substitute for it (in such a composition). Insofar as a Saussurean sign is a relation between a signifier (prototypically a word) and a signified (prototypically a concept), this means that value is again constituted by a relation (of combination or substitution) between relations (qua signifier-signified pairings) (see figure 4).

While the story is itself a sign, composed of a long combination of smaller signs (about forty sentences in all), we will focus for the time being on just one of these smaller units: a single sentence, consisting of three clauses, each of which is composed of a combination of even smaller signs (qua words, affixes, and clitics):

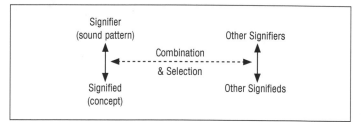

Figure 4. Selection and Combination of Signs, qua Signifier-Signified Pairings (Saussure)

Ut li winq, li ki-Ø-te-liik li r-u
and DM man DM INF-A3S-open-PSV DM E3S-eye
And the man, the one whose eyes were opened,

ki-Ø-x-ye sa' x-ch'ool,
INF-A3S-E3S-say PREP E3S-heart
said inside his heart,

"Lastima naq x-Ø-in-k'e l-in kadena oor."
shame COMP PERF-A3S-E1S-give DM-E1S chain gold
"(It's a) shame that I gave my golden chain."

As may be seen, each of the three clauses contains a verbal predicate (to be opened, to say, to give); and each of these verbal predicates is inflected. In particular, as shown in the interlinear gloss, prefixing every verb are bound morphemes, or affixes, that indicate not just the person (1st, 2nd, 3rd), number (singular or plural), and case (ergative or absolutive) of the arguments of the verb in question, but also something like tense, aspect, mood, valence, and evidentiality. For example, the first two verbs are inflected with the affix *ki-*, and the third verb is inflected with the affix *x-*. While both of these affixes indicate something like perfect aspect, *ki-* also indicates that the speaker had no direct experience of the narrated event in question; rather, it was only known to them through hearsay, reported speech, or inference. This affix is frequently used to narrate events in myths, and is often erroneously glossed as "remote past." As may be seen in the third clause, the narrator shifts from *ki-* to *x-* when reporting the words (or thoughts) of the man, qua narrated figure.

These affixes constitute two pieces of a larger paradigm, or *equivalence class*. As may be seen in figure 5 (column a), there are four other affixes in this class: *ta-* (future tense, or prospective aspect), *nak-* (habitual aspect, or nomic tense), *chi-* (optative mood, or polite imperative), and *mi-* (negative imperative). (The other three columns in figure 5 showcase all the other obligatory paradigms, qua axes of selection, that constitute transitive predicates, a particularly important axis of combination: namely, the (b) object, (c) agent, and (d) action in question.) Through a Saussurean frame, not only do each of these affixes, qua signs, constitute values; but *the class itself constitutes a somewhat more abstract value*: each of its members is relatively equivalent to the others insofar as they may all combine with the same class of

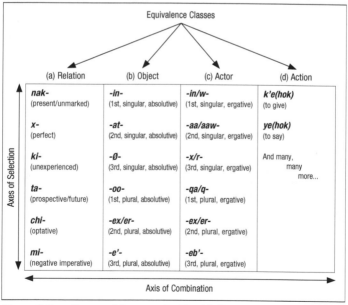

Figure 5. Paradigms and Syntagms in Q'eqchi' (So Far as They Organize Transitive Predicates)

signs (verbal predicates), and insofar as they may substitute for each other in such a slot (as prefixes of such predicates).

Such an equivalence class is a particularly important value for speakers of Q'eqchi'. Every time one uses a verbal predicate in this language, one must select one member from this class to indicate the kind of relation that exists between the world of narration and the world narrated: known or inferred (knowledge), obligated or wished (desire), nomic or prospective (time), and so forth. Returning to a key theme from the last section, these Saussurean values help constitute the relation between such worlds, and hence the relation between the actors that reside in them.

4. Inalienable Possessions

There are many other equivalence classes, and hence types of value, that lie at the base of (or serve as the infrastructure for) this sentence: not only the case paradigms marking person, number, and case; and not only lexical classes like transitive verb or noun, but also particular subtypes of such classes. In particular, and using the terminology of Benjamin Lee Whorf, there are three relatively *covert* classes of nouns on display: relatively nonpossessable items like *winq* (man); relatively alienable possessions like *kadena* (chain); and relatively inalienable possessions like *uhej* (eye) and *ch'oolej* (heart). For example, the noun *kadena* (from Spanish *cadena*) may occur with or without a possessive prefix, and undergoes no morphological changes when possessed. Most nouns in Q'eqchi', including loan words from other languages, fall into this class. In contrast, both the noun *ch'oolej* (heart) and the noun *uhej* (eye, face) typically occur in possessed form (as they do in this story); and, when not possessed, they occur with a characteristic suffix: *-(b')ej*. As may be seen in figure 6, there are about forty members of this important equivalence class: most kinship terms; many body part terms; and the words for name, place, clothing, and shadow.

Not only do the *signs* in this class have value, in a Saussurean sense; their *referents*, too, have value, in a more conventional sense. Not only are they the focus of attention and the goal of agency (as per our original definition), but they are also well-nigh priceless (in the general scheme of things). To see how, note the following claims. First, people (as wholes) are constituted by

1) Body Parts (Spatial/Temporal Relations)	
yii–b'ej	waist (in the center of)
u–hej (uu–b'ej)	eye, face (in front of, before, during, in comparison to)
e–hej	mouth (at the edge of)
sa'–ej	stomach (inside of)
ix–ej	back (in back of, after)

2) Body Parts (Appendages)	
uq'–ej	hand
oq–ej	foot
jolom–ej	head (hair)
tz'ejwal–ej	body (penis)
xolol–ej	throat
ch'ool–ej	heart

3) Non-Body Parts	
aq'–ej	clothing
na'aj–ej	place (of body, home, field)
k'ab'a'–ej	name
komun–ej	family (community, class) [< Spanish *comunidad*]

4) Marginal Members	
[ketomj] (ketomq)	domestic animals
[awimj]	seedlings
[anum–ej]	spirit [< Spanish anima]
[tib'el–ej]	body
[muh(el)–ej]	shadow, spirit
[musiq'–ej]	spirit-breath
[awab'ej, waleb'ej]	leader, president, king
[ojb'ej]	cough
[eech–ej]	possessor

5) Kinship Relations	
yuwa'–b'ej	father
na'–b'ej	mother
alal–b'ej	son (of male)
rab'in–ej	daughter (of male)
yum–b'ej	son (of female)
ko'–b'ej	daughter (of female)
yuwa'chin–b'ej	grandfather (either side), godfather
na'chin–b'ej	grandmother (either side), godmother
ii–b'ej	grandchild, great-grandchild
as–b'ej	elder brother
anab'–ej	elder sister (of male)
chaq'na'–b'ej	elder sister (of female)
iitz'in–b'ej	younger sibling
ikan–b'ej	uncle (FBr, MBr, FSiHu, MSiHu)
ikanna'–b'ej	aunt (FSi, MSi, FBrWi, MBrWi)
b'eelom–ej	husband
ixaqil–b'ej	wife
hi'–b'ej	son-in-law (DHu)
alib'–ej	daughter-in-law (SWi)
b'alk–ej	brother-in-law (SiHu of male)

Figure 6. Inalienable Possessions (qua Equivalence Class)

their inalienable possessions (as parts). For example, having introduced a person into a narrative, one can presume that others will presume that the person in question has kinship relations, body parts, clothing, and a name. Notice how odd sentences sound, even in English, when this presupposition is violated: "There was a woman who had an arm/mother/name/heart."

Second, the notion of a person is a relatively gradable entity: the more inalienable possessions something has, the more like a person it is. And many key ritual events in the life cycle of a person turn on the accrual of inalienable possessions (baptism and marriage) or their recovery when lost (illness cures). The category of a person is also a relatively distributed entity: the members of a family typically hold inalienable possessions in common: *our* house, *our* child, *our* name, and so on. And persons, qua relatively distributed entities, are highly agentive actors and salient figures in their own right, constituting instigators of action and topics of discourse.

Third, many highly animate entities have inalienable possessions, including animals and houses, gods and mountains. This makes them person-like, and easily personified in more canonical ways. For example, as instigators of action and topics of discourse, they are often attributed mental states, speech acts, and social relations.

Fourth, just as the actions of people are oriented toward caring for their inalienable possessions, their affect or mood is dependent on the condition of their inalienable possessions: when the parts flourish or founder, the whole is happy or sad. The whole strives after its parts, and any damage done to a part causes damage to the whole. The following line describes how the man felt when his sight had been restored:

Mas	naq	ki-Ø-sa-ho'		sa'	x-ch'ool	li	winq	a'an
much	COMP	INF-A3s-good-BECOME		PREP	E3s-heart	DM	man	DEIC

So much did it become good in his heart (how happy he was)

naq	x-Ø-te-li		li	r-u.
COMP	PERF-A3s-open-PSV		DM	E3s-eye

that his eyes were open.

Indeed, as this example shows, one inalienable possession in particular—the heart—is not just a body part per se, it is also the site of thought, desire, memory, feeling, conflict, decision, and intention (insofar as it is caught up in a wide variety of constructions that are used to ascribe such "mental states" to oneself and others). As the sentence beginning "Ut li winq" (And the man) showed, for example, to say something "in one's heart" is to *think* it (and not just to say it per se). And there is an important verb, *ch'oolanink*, itself derived from the word for heart, which means *to care for*.

Inalienability, then, is not just a grammatical fact (qua equivalence class of Saussurean values), but also a discursive fact, a juridical fact, a ritual fact, an existential fact, an affective fact, and, as this story shows, an ethical and economic fact as well.

Inalienable possessions, then, help constitute the subject or person (qua whole with parts), the object or value (qua topic of discourse, locus of affect, object of concern or care, and goal of action), and the cognitive and affective relations, propositional modes, or stances (that such subjects take toward such objects). This story is a case in point of this larger claim: while the narrator presumes that people have hearts and eyes, the changing state (or condition) of the latter (blinded or sighted), and the contents and transformation of the former, are the central propositions in the story. Indeed, the story itself makes narratively salient an otherwise easy to overlook, if not downright unconscious or covert, distinction between two orders of values: while the man begins and ends in a state of blindness, he comes to see the relative incommensurability—be it semantic or economic—of inalienable and alienable possessions.

Finally, note how this category of inalienable possessions, which was first noticed (and radically misunderstood) by scholars like Thorstein Veblen and Lucien Lévy-Bruhl, is not the same as the more famous one studied by Annette Weiner and highlighted by Marcel Mauss (though it includes their category, as a subcategory, to be sure). Indeed, in comparison to most of these items, Weiner's items are radically alienable in that, relatively speaking, they change hands all the time (at least through inheritance practices). Try doing that with *your hands.*

5. Aesthetic Value, Poetic Function, Equivalence Framing

We just highlighted a handful of equivalence classes in Q'eqchi', each of which consists of a set of signs (qua signifier-signified relations) that have relatively similar values insofar as they can substitute for each other (in part of a larger composition). Just as we might enlist the metalinguistic function of language to *state* facts about such classes (as I have just done), we can also enlist the poetic function of language to *show* facts about such classes (as the storyteller originally did). In particular, and following Roman Jakobson's interpretation of Saussure's categories, one key aspect of poetry involves projecting the axis of substitution onto the axis of combination, such that tokens of a common type (or signs in one and the same equivalence class) are repeated over time. And so the sentence analyzed in section 3 was a perfect example of poetry, and least in the ethnopoetics tradition inaugurated by Jakobson. In particular, three tokens of the type *clause* were repeated; and each such clause involved the repetition of tokens of even smaller types: inflectional paradigms (involving either person, number, and case, or aspect, evidence, and mood); and word classes (verb versus noun, possessable noun versus nonpossessable noun, inalienable possession versus alienable possession). And this sentence was itself a token of the type *sentence*, and hence just one instantiation of a larger construction whose concatenated repetitions constituted the story in question. Indeed, look at the last phrase of each clause, itself a possessed noun, with a shifting possessor (itself mapping onto a shifting world via the inflectional affixes we just examined): *his* eyes (*ki-*) and *his* heart (*ki-*) versus *my* golden chain (*x-*). Note, then, the relation between (1) equivalence classes and the values they embody and (2) aesthetic values more generally—such as beauty, cohesion, patterning, and (en)closure.

Indeed, the contents of this story—and, in particular, their formal cohesion and functional coherence, at least when viewed through a particular frame— help produce its very contours, such that it may be (more or less) excerpted from context as a "text," itself (relatively) alienable from its context.[1] Enclosure is as much a condition and consequence of poetic form as it is of the commodity form.

Equivalence classes are, to be sure, a much more general phenomenon than Saussure would probably have allowed: not just different affixes in the same paradigm, or different words in the same class; but also different referents of the same word, different words (or signifiers) with the same concept (or signified), different utterances of the same sentence, different versions of the same story, and different tellings of the same version. But it is also not just a linguistic phenomenon: there are different species of the same genus; different voicings of the same chord; different forms with the same function; different performers of the same character (or individuals with the same persona); different substances with the same quality; different exercises of the same power; different fonts of the same alphabet; different variables with the same value; and far, far beyond. Indeed, economists often invoke a particular type of equivalence class, the substitutable good: hamburgers for hot dogs (when you want to grill), tequila for rum (when you need to chill).

To be sure, such equivalence classes only exist within a certain *frame*: what other chords (or chord voicings) can substitute for Gm7 in *this* composition (to *these* ears, in *this* era, according to *this* tradition, within *this* world, etcetera). Insofar as such frames are context-dependent, then modes of equivalence, with their foregrounding of different kinds of similarities and differences, are as well. And sameness and difference are themselves gradient phenomena (more or less the same and more or less different, along what dimensions and to what degree), with contingent thresholds (what counts as similar *enough* [to whom], what counts as *too* different [and why]) (see figure 7). And hence there are usually a politics and a pragmatics underlying any such poetics.

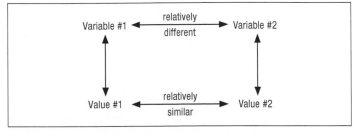

Figure 7. Equivalence qua Variation with Invariance

6. Chickens, Machetes, and Chains: Meta-equivalence and the Purification of Value

Speakers of Q'eqchi' not only *show* most of the foregoing modes of equivalence in their mundane practices, they also utilize specific linguistic resources for *stating* various modes of equivalence. While, in some sense, any sign (word or concept) projects an equivalence class (in particular, the set of referents that could be referred to by that word, or captured with that concept), certain words, or linguistic constructions more generally, *conceptualize equivalence per se*. And such constructions are often quite telling about local understandings of value and, in particular, its political contestation and historical transformation.

As a case in point, the meaning of a wide variety of words in Q'eqchi' may be analogically changed by combining them with one of two other words: either *kaxlan* (chicken/foreign) or *ch'iich'* (machete/metallic). For example, if *aatin* means word or language, *kaxlan aatin* means the Spanish language; if *ulul* means brains, *ulul ch'iich'* means computer; if *mokooch* refers to a large leaf, *kaxlan mokooch* refers to an umbrella; if *bajlaq* refers to a corncob, *baqlaq ch'iich'* refers to a bus (or bicycle).

Such constructions not only enable speakers to refer to newer objects using older terms; they also enable them to simultaneously indicate similarity (of form or function) and difference (in origin or artificer). One entity (an airplane) becomes both an analog and an alter of the other (a vulture). In this way, such constructions project a three-fold *ontology of values* onto all such referents: first, relatively indigenous entities versus nonindigenous entities; and, within the class of nonindigenous entities, relatively metallic versus nonmetallic entities (see figure 8). More pointedly, if *kaxlan* is often used in compound constructions that refer to colonizers (and their ideas, customs, and signs), *ch'iich'* is typically used in compound constructions to refer to the commodities of those colonizers.

Again, then, we have values in a larger-than-linguistic sense: for many such objects are, if not pursued and preferred as goods, at least denigrated and avoided as bads. Moreover, moving from the value of the signifieds to the value of signifiers, such linguistic constructions are themselves valued, at least by some speakers, over Spanish loan words that might otherwise take their place. For example, some language purists would like to replace words like *computadora* (computer) with constructions like *ulul ch'iich'* (metallic brain), and thereby purge the language of Spanish influence.

While the story itself does not have any tokens of either such marked constructions, it certainly has several

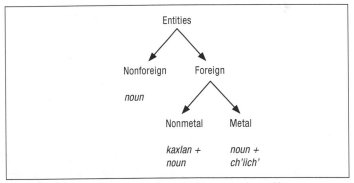

Figure 8. Compound Constructions and Meta-equivalence Classes

Spanish words that have been loaned, including *kadena oro*, or "chain [of] gold," and *Dios*, or "God." Indeed, when *kadena* first appears in the story it is identical to its Spanish equivalent. Only in its last occurrence, when it is part of a reported speech utterance said by the man, is it (partially) assimilated to the phonology of Q'eqchi'. In particular, the penultimate vowel is lengthened and the final vowel is lost: *kadena* becomes *kadeen*.

It should also be stressed that *oro* (gold, from Spanish *oro*), itself assimilated to Q'eqchi' phonology as *oor* in one token, like *plaat* (silver, < Spanish *plata*), contrasts with *ch'iich'*, in that it means a special kind of precious metal (gold) as opposed to nonprecious metals (typically iron or steel). Interestingly, there is a relatively high occurrence of Spanish loan words in the text, words for which there have long been Q'eqchi' equivalents. For example, the Q'eqchi' word *q'ol* would normally be used to refer to necklaces or chains (and also, interestingly, to rust, and even to sap). And it often connotes a relatively cheap piece of jewelry (insofar as it is made out of a less precious metal and, in particular, one more likely to rust). And even the word *kadena* itself was long ago well assimilated into Q'eqchi' as *kareen* (for there is no sound /d/ in Q'eqchi'); whereas the storyteller here uses minimally assimilated variants. Certain elements of the story, then, managed to slip through the sieve of a local language ideology, having been minimally purified of Spanish influence.

In short, not only is the man's golden chain an alienable possession (in contrast to his eyes), it is also referred to with a minimally transformed Spanish construction, such that not just its high value, but also its being foreign—and hence its being *alien* in addition to its being *alienable*—is foregrounded, and thereby made aesthetically significant.

7. Singularities, Replacements, Commodities (and Something Else Entirely)

As another example of a lexically instantiated equivalence class that makes reflexive reference to equivalence per se (through its conceptual logic, or sense), we might take the word *eeqaj*, which is usually best translated as "replacement." It refers to activities as disparate as house-building, civil-religious elections, vengeance, loans, illness cures, adultery, and namesakes (see figure 9). Such practices involve the substitution of one entity for another entity, insofar as these entities have shared properties, and insofar as they hold a role in an obligatory position. For example, one man may substitute his labor for another man's labor insofar as men have similar degrees of strength and skill, and insofar as a position in a labor pool must be filled. And an effigy of a sick person may substitute for that person in an illness cure insofar as they have inalienable possessions in common (such as hair and clothing), and insofar as a divinity requires one or the other as compensation. In all such cases, entities and actors within certain domains *must* have a replacement (lest their role go unfulfilled, their function stay unserved, or some imbalance be maintained); and other entities *may* substitute for such entities (insofar as they are judged relatively equivalent in regard to their quantities of particular qualities). All such entities constitute values (what signs stand for, what agents strive for), and their periodic replenishment through practices of replacement has long constituted a large part of village economies.

Indeed, the word *eeqaj* is frequently used to refer to use values of a more quotidian sort. For example, when firewood is used up, the roof wears out, or a battery goes dead, one can gather, build, or buy their "replacement." In this framing, the equivalence classes underlying replacement strongly contrast with the equivalence classes underlying two more famous kinds of values, typically known as singularities and commodities

---

Replacing a Person in Some Kind of Office

1. A newly elected village mayor is called the replacement (*eeqaj*) of the previous mayor.

2. In the religious hierarchy, or *cofradía*, a newly elected married couple (mertoom) is called the replacement of the previous couple.

3. In cases where a boy is given the name of his father, he would be considered his father's replacement.

Settling Some Kind of Score

4. One man's vengeful action toward another man is called the replacement of the other man's prior insulting or harmful action.

5. One soccer team's tying goal is called the replacement of the other team's previous goal.

6. A man who took another man's place within a labor pool, or fulfilled another man's more solitary labor obligations, is called the latter man's replacement.

7. The money returned to another as the settling of a loan is called the replacement of the originally loaned money.

8. In cases where a person has suffered fright (xiwajenaq, or "susto"), as brought on by a moral breech such as forgetting to pray or deprecating maize, they could bury a replacement, or effigy, of themselves in the place where they were frightened. Only in this way could the person not fall ill, insofar as the agency that frightened them accepted the effigy as a replacement for the person's health.

9. A man who slept with another man's wife is called his replacement.

Replenishing a Worn-Out or Used-Up Good

10. A newly built house is called the replacement of the owner's old house.

11. Most generally, the accidental loss or normal provisioning of a necessary item entails a replacement. Such processes often involve the most stereotypical use values: a bag of salt, a lantern's worth of oil, a set of batteries, a pair of rubber boots, and so forth.

Figure 9. Types of Replacement (eeqaj)*, a Mode of Meta-equivalence* (see figure 10). In particular, rather than asking whether these are instances of the same individual (Is that the golden chain your mother left you?), or use values with the same exchange value (Does one golden chain cost as much as two acres of cloud forest?), we ask whether my golden chain and your golden chain are similar in quantity and quality: Do they have similar enough degrees of the same key dimensions (e.g., their weight, luster, shape, or carat), such that one could replace the other (in regard to some function)?

As will be shown, all three of these equivalence classes (singularities, replacements, commodities) are particularly salient in the context of this story, insofar as none of them really captures the relation between golden chains and sighted eyes. The logic of offerings

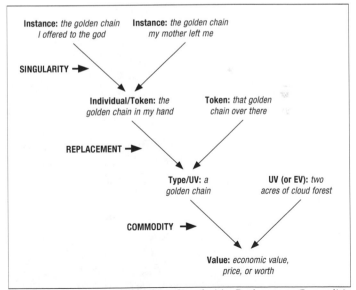

Figure 10. Three Kinds of Equivalence: Singularities, Replacements, Commodities

is altogether otherwise; such that this lack of capture (qua nonequivalence with any of these three large-scale equivalence classes) is itself illuminating.

8. The Translation of Equivalence: Value, Sense, Path

While we have just been focusing on a very wide sense of equivalence, and on its lexical instantiation in several important Q'eqchi' constructions, the definition easily includes more stereotypical variants. For example, in translation, expressions from different languages are treated as having similar meanings (*el gato* means "the cat"); in paraphrase, different expressions from the same language are treated as having similar meanings (a *noob* is something like a naive novice). Similar issues pertain to different domains. For example, there is something like translation and paraphrase not just in the realm of currency (one US dollar equals 0.89 euro, or 100 US cents), but also in the domain of measurement (one pound equals 2.2 kilograms, or 16 ounces).

We end with these admittedly trivial examples of "translation" in order to return to Saussurean value proper. To do this, one should note the relation, if not relative equivalence (!), between (1) Saussure's distinction between value (*valeur*) and significance (*signifié*, also variously translated as "meaning," "signified," or "signification") and (2) Gottlob Frege's distinction between sense (*Sinn*) and referent (*Bedeutung*) (see figure 11). For example, while *Hillary's husband* and

Chelsea's father (as two linguistic expressions, or signs) might have the same significance or referent (say, a particular man named Bill), they have different values or senses. To find out whom the first expression refers to, or signifies, you need to know who Hillary is, and what a husband is. To find out whom the second expression refers to, or signifies, you need to know who Chelsea is, and what a father is. (Note, by the way, the role of inalienable possessions, like proper names and kinship terms, in guiding interpreters from messages to referents.) While they may get to the same destination (qua referent), they take very different paths to get there (qua sense). And so while they have the same significance, such that one could be used to translate the other, they have different values. Similarly, while English *you* and Spanish *tú* might have the same significance in some utterance (in that they could both refer to one and the same addressee), they have very different values in that *tú* belongs to a larger paradigm, or equivalence class, that includes *usted* (and, in some dialects of Spanish, *vos*), not to mention the plural forms *ustedes* and *vosotros*. Finally, while the English sentence offered in section 3 was a reasonable equivalent of the Q'eqchi' sentence, a quick glance at the interlinear translation,

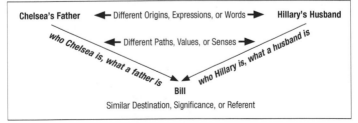

Figure 11. Sense and Referent (Frege), Value and Significance (Saussure)

or a careful read of my description of the grammatical categories in question, shows that the two sentences constitute (and incorporate) radically different values.

Equivalence of reference (or signification) is relatively shallow, and easy to come by, in comparison to equivalence of sense (or value). The latter is much more difficult to achieve and perceive, and hence constitutes a much scarcer good, or greater value, as it were. Part of the reason Saussure was so valuable is that he understood value as equivalence of relations (or paths, or sense) rather than as equivalence of relata (or destinations, qua referents). And he offered a method for securing (in our translations and interpretations), or at least showcasing (in our grammars and ethnographies), such valuable relations between relations. As these last five sections should have shown, his often-invoked comparison of economic and linguistic value was, in effect, a red herring—one gobbled up (and regurgitated) by enthusiasts and critics alike—as the relations mediating linguistic and economic orders are much more subtle and pervasive.

9. Possible Worlds: From Saussure's Value to Frege's Sense (and Truth Value)

Let's return to the story, picking up where we left off in section 3. Speaking of the golden chain that he gave to Lord Chajul, the man says inside his heart:

"A'an mas terto   x-tz'aq.
DEIC   very expensive E3s-price
"It is very expensive.

"X-Ø-in-k'e   raj jun li   mayej mas kub'enaq x-tz'aq
PERF-A3s-E1s-give CF   one DM   offer very cheap   E3s-price
"I could have given a very cheap offering

    "ut   x-Ø-teli   tana li   w-u."
    and   PERF-A3s-be_opened   AF   DM   E1s-eye
    "and my eyes would probably (still) have been opened."

A lot happens in these lines. Notice that a comparison is being made between the offering that was actually given (the golden chain) and an offering that could have been given (something else entirely). While the price of the former was very high, the price of the latter could have been very low. Notice that the man discursively draws out the causal connection between the offering he made (the golden chain) and what he received in return (the opening of his eyes). And notice that the man is hypothesizing that a different cause or "path" (giving a cheap offering rather than the expensive one) could have resulted in the same effect or "destination." (Note, then, how something like a sense-referent distinction is mediated by the relation between possible actions, not just the relation between possible signs.) In effect, he presupposes that an offering must be made (to get the return); and he proposes that the offering could have differed in its relative degree (low versus high) of a key dimension: *price.*

Notice that, to do all this, the man leaves off speaking of the actual world, and begins speaking of possible worlds. The first clause of the line beginning "X-Ø-in-k'e raj" (I could have given), functioning like the antecedent of a conditional construction (*if p*), is modalized with the counterfactual operator *raj*: it specifies a world that is counter to the actual world; that is, the clause in question describes a state of affairs that is contrary to what actually occurred (in the story itself). The line's second clause, which functions like the consequent of a conditional construction (*then q*), is modalized with the afactive operator *tana*: it specifies what *probably* would have happened in such a counterfactual world. And notice that all this happens in a world of reported speech: the teller of the tale (in our world, some fifty years ago) recounts the actions of the man, and some of these actions include his speech actions (like these two sentences here). Such speech actions describe not only past (or perfected) actual events (relative to where the man stands in time); they also describe past counterfactual actions and their probable consequences (from where the man stands in thought).

Note, by the way, that one does not need to go to modern financial markets to find calculative actions, risky propositions, leveraged assets, modalized contracts, and the concatenations of possible worlds. They lie at the heart of everyday utterances; indeed, according to speakers of Q'eqchi', they lie inside our very own hearts.

10. Reworded Possibilities: From Imagining Outcomes to Second-Guessing Actions

Marx liked to talk about man's (allegedly) unique ability to imagine the world before he makes it. Just as important, we see here, is our ability to second-guess a (trans) action after we've undertaken it. Indeed, in these two lines we see how speakers of Q'eqchi' publicly represent such (seemingly) private representations. Crucially, such a misgiving or post-hoc machination does not just occur (in the text) as a real-time thought process. A few lines later in the story, when the man has become blind again, he himself captures the gist of what he just did by (indirectly) reporting his prior speech to his present self, such that both the sense of what he said, and the expression by which he said it, remain only relatively invariant:

"K'a'   naq   x-Ø-in-ye
why/what   COMP   PERF-A3S-E1S-say
"Why did I say

   "naq ha' li   kadeen mas terto   x-tz'aq
   COMP TOP DM chain   very expensive E3S-price
   "that the chain was very expensive

      "ke   chi-r-u   li   w-u?"
      COMP PREP-E3S-RN DM   E1S-eye
      "in comparison to my eyes?"

         chan-Ø-Ø
         say-PRES-A3S
         he said

           naq   ki-Ø-r-eek'a'
           COMP   INF-A3S-E3S-feel
           when he felt

naq   ink'a'   chik   na'-Ø-ilok.
COMP   NEG   more   PRES-A3s-see
that he could no longer see.

Note again the poetic enchaining of clauses (headed by complementizers). Note that the first four clauses are the man's reinterpretation of his own words from earlier lines. While they capture the essence of what he said and/or the effect of what he did, they are not exactly equivalent. In particular, here he makes an explicit comparison between the price of the chain and his eyes; whereas in the earlier lines he only implicitly compared an expensive offering with a cheap offering, hypothesizing that the latter might have yielded the same return. In paraphrasing his own thoughts, he distinctly transformed the sense of what was originally expressed.

11. The Wording and Worlding of Truth Value

Let me repeat two key lines of this last long sentence (in slightly altered form), insofar as they show a canonical example of the comparative construction in Q'eqchi:

i. mas terto   x-tz'aq   li   kadeen chi-r-u   li   w-u

ii. very expensive E3S-price DM chain   PREP-E3S-RN DM E1S-eye

iii. "The chain is very expensive relative to (literally, in the eye/face of) my eyes."

iv. ⟦the chain is very expensive relative my eyes⟧^{w} =
∃d[the-chain is d-expensive ∧ d > OG(my eyes)$_{cost}$ + *mas*]

v. In the world (w) at issue, there exists a degree (d), the chain is expensive to that degree, and that degree is greater than the degree to which "my eyes" are expensive by *a significant amount.*

As before, the first line (i) is a sentence in Q'eqchi' (broken up into words and affixes); the second line (ii) is an interlinear gloss of the morphemes in question; and the third line (iii) provides an English translation. The fourth line (iv) represents the truth conditions for the Q'eqchi' sentence using a simplified and slightly idiosyncratic version of lambda calculus (a particularly useful and elegant logical notation). And the last line (v) spells out, in "plain English," what the expression in this logical notation actually means.

By specifying the truth conditions for the sentence in question, these lines thereby specify what the world would have to be like—or at least believed to be like—for the sentence to be assigned a positive (as opposed to a negative) *truth value.* To return to our initial characterization of value: not only are truth values precisely what declarative sentences stand for, or denote (in a certain widespread paradigm of linguistics), but they are also—at least in the eyes of many collectivities—precisely what agents (should) strive for.

To assign a truth value to an utterance, and thereby evaluate it, requires that we be able to check the world to see if, indeed, the truth conditions of that utterance are satisfied. Crucially, as may be seen by the superscripted *w* in line iv, the truth value of such an utterance is not to be evaluated in *any* world, but rather only in the world *about which* someone is speaking (or thinking). And that world is often accessible only in relation to the world *in which* someone is speaking. Indeed, as we saw above, the man didn't actually utter this sentence per se. Rather, this sentence was his own paraphrase of what he had said or thought earlier in the story (akin to indirectly reported self-speech); and this paraphrase was itself embedded, at least three times over, in a series of other worlds (indicated by means of reported speech or thought):

(In our world, some fifty years ago from today) the nameless narrator said₁
    [that (in the world of the story) the man thought (or "said inside his heart")₂
        [why did I say₃ (at some time prior to this moment)
            [that the chain is very expensive in comparison to my eyes]]].

Reported speech is one way we shift worlds, and thereby shift the conditions under which the truth values of sentences are evaluated. (And simply telling stories is another: *in the world of this story*, a blind man makes a pilgrimage to Lord Chajul.) As we saw in our discussion of conditional constructions, counterfactual and afactual operators, like the clitics *raj* and *tana*, are another way. Operators expressing deontic modality, indicating what one *may* or *may not* do, *should* and *should not* do, are another. Recall our discussion of the inflectional affixes *mi-* and *chi-*, in section 3, which are often used performatively (and more or less politely) to establish modes of obligation and permission. And, as will be shown in section 26, Mauss's account of the gift, and A. Mitchell Innes's account of money and debt, describe yet other ways of deontically establishing and regimenting worlds.

    Indeed, anthropology itself has long been devoted to ethnography: a seminal technique for evaluating—by both ferreting out and spelling out—the truth conditions and, more generally, satisfaction conditions, of other worlds (in and through the words [and worlds] of others). For example, *in the world of the Q'eqchi'* (or at least one such world, for there are infinitely many), *you should give with all your heart.* In the last three sections we have been interested in the methods we use to learn about such worlds (and the values they incorporate), as well as the poetic and pragmatic techniques agents use to establish, organize, rank, demote, invert, and move between such worlds. I'll leave it to readers to debate the reality, and relative value, of the worlds themselves.

12. Commensuration and Comparison

Let's take a closer look at the last sentence, which showed a canonical instance of the comparative construction in Q'eqchi'. As may be seen in lines i–iii, such constructions involve a range of components. There is the figure of comparison (the chain), a ground of comparison (the man's eyes), a dimension of comparison (price), a direction of comparison (greater than), and a magnitude of comparison (very or much), indicated by the form *mas* (see figure 12). In particular, the figure is said to have a much higher degree of the dimension at issue than the ground. Crucially, to compare a figure and a ground in this way is to presuppose that the figure and ground are commensurate (in one important sense of this word): they each have *some* degree—but not necessarily the *same* degree—of the dimension at issue (such that they may be compared in the first place). Indeed, it is, in part, precisely this presupposition (that sighted eyes have a price, just like golden chains) that causes the god to return the man's chain (and take back his sight). Needless to say, the

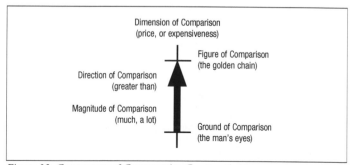

Figure 12. Components of Comparative Construction

dimensions underlying comparative constructions, and assessments of gradation more generally, are often key values. And comparison per se, as a mode of evaluation, is a fundamental act in the creation and expression of value.

As showcased in this example, the ground of comparison is the argument of an adposition (*chiru*), which is itself composed of three parts: the preposition *chi* (indicating a relation of some kind); the possessive prefix *r-* (cross-referencing the possessor of the relational noun, in this case the man's eyes); and the relational noun *-u* (itself originally derived from the same inalienable possession that is used to refer to eyes or faces, but here semantically bleached to mean something like front surface). Body parts often play such dual roles in a language. Compare, for example, "my back" and "in back of me." Thus, while I gloss this construction as "relative to," it could also be more literally translated as "in the eyes (or face) of," and felicitously translated as "in comparison to," or even "in confrontation with" (though, to be sure, all such English constructions have different Saussurean values). Note, then, the important role played by such an inalienable possession: not only does it serve as the ground of comparison (in this particular utterance), it also plays a key role in the comparative construction itself (whatever the ground, figure, or dimension in question).

Note, then, the radical reflexivity underlying what first appears to be a relatively straightforward story (and recall the wordplay from section 1: "when he saw that his eyes could see"). Such self-reflexivity is perhaps the highest of Q'eqchi' aesthetic values. In a more canonical myth, for example, which describes the elopement of the sun and the moon, and the creation of the cosmos more generally, not only is the sun a narrated figure, whose actions help constitute the world, but his very movements in the story constitute the temporal background against which all the narrated events unfold. In later sections of this essay, the Mayan penchant for self-reflexive storytelling (or world-making) will be leveraged to theorize the constitution of the values described in the story through the movement of the story itself—its tellings and retellings, its significations and interpretations, and thus not just its further extension into the space-time of some particular world, but also its extension into (and out of) more and more distal worlds (including, as should now be clear, our own).

13. The Genealogy of Intensity, the Revaluation of Value

Without the intensifier *mas* such a comparative construction would indicate that the figure exceeds the ground (with respect to its degree of the dimension at issue) by some amount, large or small. With *mas*, such a construction indicates that the figure does not just exceed the ground (in its degree of the dimension at issue), but that it exceeds it by a *significant amount* (+ *mas*). *Mas*, then, changes the magnitude of comparison or intensity of degree. Crucially, what counts as a significant amount is dependent on the dimension in question, the type of figure and ground being compared, and other features of the speech event. For example, the difference in price between an expensive gold chain and a very expensive gold chain is much larger than the difference in price between an expensive chicken and a very expensive chicken.

The intensifier *mas* is itself a loan word from Spanish, where it plays a role similar to English *-er/ more* (and *most*). Note, then, that whereas Spanish *más* marks direction (*more* as opposed to *less*), Q'eqchi' *mas* indicates magnitude (*a lot* more as opposed to *a little* more, or *very* expensive, as opposed to *somewhat* expensive). Its Saussurean value, or Fregean sense, has been substantially transformed. Q'eqchi' has long had a host of other words for indicating intensity, and magnitude more generally. Such forms constitute an equivalence class: while they all have slightly different meanings, they can all serve as differential operators in comparative constructions, thereby indicating the magnitude of difference in degree between figures and grounds.

While all such signs have interesting histories, and hence changing Saussurean values, two stand out in particular. *Xiikil* is usually translated as "abundante, mucho, bastante."[2] While not usually considered a loan word, I suspect it was borrowed from Nahuatl, the language spoken by the Aztecs. Frances Karttunen, for example, defines the Nahuatl word *xiquipilli* as "purse, pouch, sack/costal, talega, alforja o borsa"; and she says, "This is used symbolically in the vigesimal counting system to represent the unit 'eight thousand.'"[3] There is good evidence that the Nahuatl word *xiquipil* was used by speakers of Q'eqchi' in Alta Verapaz, at least in the 1600s and 1700s, to count cacao beans. These beans functioned as a kind of currency at the time, and could also be given by the Q'eqchi' to Dominican friars or state officials to pay tribute or taxes. According to Laura Caso Barrera and Mario Aliphat Fernández, for example, in 1786 an ax could be (forcibly) exchanged for one xiquipil.[4] That is, if a friar or state official offered you an ax, you were obligated to give them eight thousand cocoa beans in return. I suspect, then, that a word (*xiquipilli*) that originally referred to a large sack (or the number 8,000 = 20 x 20 x 20) in Nahautl, was "borrowed" (perhaps forcibly) into Q'eqchi' as *xiquipil*, with a similar meaning; and this same word, with some phonological change (*xiikil*), came to be used as a differential operator and amount quantifier, indicating a large but indeterminate magnitude (rather than a precise number or an explicit unit per se). Interestingly, perhaps owing to its accursed history, utterances involving this word often have negative connotations, in that they don't just indicate "many" or "much," but also "too much" or "too many," and hence an excessive amount.

The case of *jwal*, which is often glossed as *mas mas* (that is, as *mas* reduplicated, and hence iconically intensified), is even more interesting. In effect, an inalienable possession meaning "king" or "ruler" became the word for "power" or "might," which became a degree-marking adverb with a meaning similar to "very, very" or "a whole lot." Let me briefly lay out some of the key steps in this process. It looks like there used to be an inalienable possession *waleb'ej*, which meant lord, king, or leader. (Recall the "marginal members" in the table in figure 6.) In a sixteenth-century will, for example, we get the expression *aj gwaleb'j*, which Robert Burkitt translated as "person of worship or authority, headman, etc."[5] The form *aj*, which accompanies the inalienable possession in this example, has long functioned as a status designator, or agent classifier: indicating that the noun it modifies is (prototypically) a human male. I suspect that this inalienable possession (without its suffix), along with this status designator, was reanalyzed as *ajwal*. For example, in a seventeenth-century petition analyzed by Ray Freeze,[6] it looks like *ajwal* (sometimes spelled *ahual*) functioned as a noun (or perhaps an attributive adjective): *Dios ca-nim-ahual* (god E1P-big-lord), or "God, our great lord." It looks like *-aj(a)wal* then became an obligatorily possessed noun meaning something like power or greatness. For example, in William Sedat's dictionary we find the possessed form *-ajacual*.[7] This form could occur before a noun, itself cross-referenced by the possessive prefix *r-*. For example, *r-ajacual cuinq* (his-powerfulness man, or "hombre poderoso"). This same form also seemed to function as a degree-marking adverb in front of adjectives. For example, in the same dictionary, we find the construction *rajacual us*, translated as "muy bueno" (very good).[8] This last type of function, increased in intensity or degree (perhaps through its contrast with *mas*) was carried over into the present form, *jwal* (very, very; a whole lot), which looks like it is a phonological reduction of the longer construction. There is, then, *a deep relation between inalienability, sovereignty, and intensity.*

Notice, then, the radical revaluation of Saussurean values (not to mention truth values, exchange values, use values, and moral values) that all this implies (see figure 13). In this way, language history can be wielded as genealogy in the Nietzschean sense: To study the processes that impose new meanings on prior signs, new functions on prior forms, new forms on prior substances, new identities (moralities, values, ethics, etc.) on prior

---

Key Steps in the Transformation of *Mas*

Spanish *más* (more, most) > Q'eqchi' *mas* (very, much/many) via reanalysis and borrowing

Q'eqchi' *mas* (very, much/many) > Q'eqchi' *jwal* (very, very much/many) via "purification"

Key Steps in the Transformation of *Xiikil*

Nahuatl *xiquipilli* (8,000, sack of cacao beans) > Q'eqchi' *xiquipil* (8,000, sack) via borrowing

Q'eqchi' *xiquipil* (8,000, sack) > Q'eqchi' *xiikil* (very large amount, excessive amount) via abstraction

Key Steps in the Transformation of *Jwal*

wal(e)-b'ej (leader-IP; originally an inalienable possession, meaning lord, king, or leader)

aj (SD; originally a status designator, indicating (prototypically) male, human agent)

aj wal (SD lord) > *ajwal* (lord, king) via reanalysis

-ajwal (lord, king) > *-ajwal* (power, might) via semantic abstraction

r-ajwal noun (E3S-power noun) > *rajwal noun* (powerful noun) via reanalysis

rajwal (powerful) via semantic abstraction > *rajwal* (very; very, very) via semantic abstraction

raj(a)wal (very; very, very) > *jwal* (very; very, very) via phonological reduction

Figure 13. On the Genealogy of Intensity, or Revaluation of Saussurean Values

individuals, new conventions (codes, grammars, laws, felicity conditions, or norms) on prior collectivities; and especially *the counterprocesses*, and their consequences for forms of life and, as will be shown in the next two sections, modes of consciousness.

14. Semiotic Values

In a Peircean tradition, semiotic processes may be understood as consisting of three components: a sign (whatever stands for something else); an object (whatever is stood for by a sign); and an interpretant (whatever a sign creates insofar as it is taken to stand for an object). For example, and perhaps most simply, a student raises her hand (sign), indicating a desire to ask a question (object), and the teacher calls on her (interpretant). More relevantly, a man makes a request and gives an offering (sign), indicating his desire for a miracle and his belief in a god's power (object), and Lord Chajul restores his sight (interpretant). More canonically, my recounting in English of a story in Q'eqchi' relates to that story as interpretant to sign, where the object in question consists of all the actions and events so described. Returning to section 11, just as line v was a plain English interpretant of line iv, itself an expression in a logical notation, lines iv and v, along with lines ii and iii, were interpretants of line i, itself an expression in a Mayan language. Finally, and perhaps most intuitively, this entire essay is not just an interpretant (qua exegesis or "interpretation") of that story, it is also an interpretant of (snippets of) stories told by Aristotle and Marx, Saussure and Frege, Nietzsche and Peirce, among others. From this standpoint, meaning—or semiotic value—is not a relation between a sign and an interpretant (nor a relation between a signifier and a signified, qua sign and object). Rather, as seen in figure 14, it is again constituted by a relation between relations: the relation between the interpretant and the object relates to, or corresponds with, the relation between the object and the sign.

Semiotic processes relate to value in multiple ways. Recall our first definition of value: that which lies at the intersection of what agents strive for and what signs stand for. Not only are objects (in the semiotic sense) precisely what signs stand for, but signs often relate to interpretants (and interpretants relate to objects) as means to ends. For example, the man gave an offering (sign), *in order to* have his eyes healed (interpretant), and *by means of* indicating his desires and beliefs (object). And the story itself was recounted, I presume, to portray a world, inform an addressee, teach a moral, navigate an ethical dilemma, showcase the speaker's competence or virtue, earn a wage, entertain a guest, make a comparison, manage a social relation, return a favor, while away the time, and maybe even quell a rebellion or convert a soul (as will be shown in section 21).

Recall our second definition of value: a relation between agents (think signer and interpreter, qua man and god) mediated by a relation between entities (think

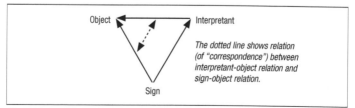

Figure 14. Core Components of Semiotic Processes

sign and interpretant, qua giving of chain and granting of sight). To be sure, the social relations in question don't have to belong to the signer and interpreter per se. As we saw in section 3, a sign-object relation can mediate the relation between those who signify and those who are signified. And an interpretant-object relation can mediate the relation between those spoken to (or addressed) and those spoken about (or described) (see figure 15). And so forth. Needless to say, expressing, maintaining, creating, and transforming social relations are themselves key values (qua end), typically undertaken by engaging in semiotic processes (qua means). As Bronislaw Malinowski knew so well, such modes of *semiotic labor* constitute a large part of life itself, qua *sociality*.

Recall our third definition of value: the value of a Saussurean sign (qua signifier-signified pairing) is constituted by its capacity to combine with, and substitute for,

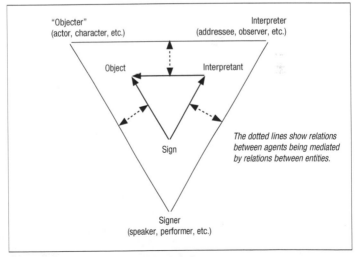

Figure 15. Social Relations and Semiotic Processes

other such signs (within some system of signs). While Saussurean semiological structures might at first seem orthogonal to Peircean semiotic processes, they are easily incorporated. First, don't confuse Saussure's sign with Peirce's sign. Rather, the most appropriate mapping between the two analytics is arguably as follows: signifier is to signified as sign is to object. And second, just as one can investigate Saussurean values through relatively abstract structural oppositions, one may also investigate them through relatively concrete eventive sequencings. (Recall, for example, our discussion of the poetic function of language in section 5.) That is, the value of any sign (object or interpretant) is constituted by its ability to combine with, substitute for, or simply relate to, other signs (objects or interpretants) within an action, sequence, or assemblage (see figure 16).

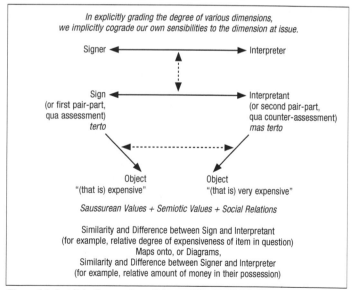

Figure 16. Implicit Comparison of Agents Who Explicitly Compare Entities

For example, it is often useful to think of the object of a sign as a correspondence-preserving projection from all interpretants of that sign, insofar as such interpretants are enabled and constrained, or allowed and prohibited, by some range of mediating (regimenting or "sanctioning") agents, be those agents human or nonhuman, lively or nonlively, institutionally or infrastructurally realized, virtual or imagined (see figure 17, which focuses narrowly on semantic regimentation via interpreting agents [qua translators]). Indeed, a key agent mediating the interpretants of a sign is very often the object of that sign (or one of its parts), understood not as a referent or signification, or even as an objectification, but rather as an "objection." For just because worlds are represented, and indeed radically constituted through their representation, doesn't mean that they aren't very, very *real*.

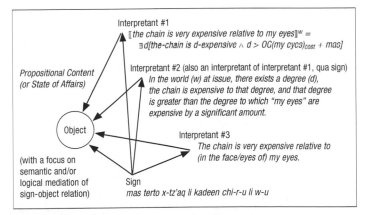

Figure 17. Semantic Regimentation of Sign-Object Relation via Linguistic and Logical Relationality

15. The Regimentation and Internalization of Value

Crucially, many semiotic agents can internalize (some portion of) the possible interpretants of their signs, and come to act accordingly. All life-forms, arguably, do this on evolutionary timescales. And human agents, and the collectivities they belong to, are particularly good at doing this on historical, biographical, and interactional timescales. For example, this essay, as my interpretant of the story, can only range so far (given some such regime of regimentation or sanctioning). And I myself have regimented or, more generally, mediated my interpretant of the story (that is, the writing of this essay) in light of the possible interpretants of it (as a sign), by members of a much larger public (down the line), so far as I have experienced their reactions (in the past) or can imagine or predict their reactions (in the future). This public includes not only speakers of Q'eqchi', friends from my fieldsite, and linguists of Mesoamerican languages; but also members of my discipline, readers of this essay, the editors of this press, and even my own mother (with her withering criticism and blood-red pen).

Such facts are also integral to this story, and its creation and communication of value, in the following ways. First, in thinking (or saying in his heart) that he could have given a less expensive good and still have received the same return, the man was regimented, or sanctioned, by Lord Chajul: the offering was returned, and his sight was taken away. So, in part, the reversal of the exchange was the god's interpretant of, or response to, the man's relatively private sign—saying, in effect, *thou shall not* think like that (calculate like that, misgive like that). Second, upon hearing a story like this, people might come to internalize the actions of Lord Chajul (in particular, his interpretant of the man's misgivings). And those people might thereby come to modulate their own behaviors accordingly (as if Lord Chajul might intercept the conversations they have with themselves, in their hearts, about what they could have offered instead).

Nietzsche and Freud, not to mention Bentham and Foucault, famously theorized the self's internalization of values, through the regimentation of its value-oriented actions and thoughts by external agents (even if only imagined), and the role this played in the creation of self-reflexivity. And the nameless narrator here seems to think that similar facts apply to "us," as regimented by "God." That is, we can internalize the main value communicated by the story, and thereby come to reflexively regiment our own actions (in its image, or under its sign) without actually having to be regimented in the world of fact. Our recognition of the man's regimentation in *that* world may be more than enough to transform how we behave in *this* one.

16. From Figures to Grounds: Labor Power and Semiotic Potential

We have been examining value across a wide range of framings. Within each frame, there is something like a figure-ground distinction. For example, rather than focus on the relation between objects of exchange, focus on that relation in relation to the relations between agents of exchange. Rather than focus on signifier-signified relations, focus on relations of combination and substitution among such relations. Rather than focus on equivalence per se (difference of variables with sameness of values), focus on framings of equivalence, which themselves determine which variables and values are relevant, and what counts as relative sameness and difference. Rather than focus on referents (qua destination), focus on sense (qua path); and rather than focus on sense-referent relations in world-independent ways, focus on their world-specific mediation, and on the ways actors not only shift among already existing worlds but also create new worlds through practices of worlding (themselves tightly coupled to practices of wording). Rather than focus on qualia (or qualities), focus on the comparative grounds and implicit intensities (or degrees) underlying comparative strategies. Rather than focus on the comparative construction per se, as an essential resource for evaluation, focus on the genealogy of the signs that constitute it, and hence the relation between intensity and history, power and degree, dimension and magnitude. Rather than focus on signifier-signified relations, and virtual structures and actual assemblages of such relations, focus on interpretant-object relations in relation to object-sign relations, and hence on the temporal unfolding of semiotic processes per se. And rather than focus on the unfolding of semiotic processes, focus on how they are regimented by "objects," and the ways such regimentation is internalized by "subjects." In short, while value might come to the fore through the appearance of such figures, to really understand its conditions and consequences one must attend to such grounds.

Indeed, we can take this process one step further: rather than focus on semiotic processes, focus on *the grounds of semiosis*. Let me explain. In one sense, signs, objects, and interpretants are values as per our original characterization (however provisional). In another sense, the relations between relations that organize semiotic processes (by interrelating signs, objects, and interpretants) are semiotic values as per the arguments of section 14. Crucially, however, semiotic processes only precede in reference to an even more original (tacit, diffuse, distributed, or abstract) ensemble of values. Or, rather, semiotic processes, and their component parts, only appear as (valuable) figures in reference to a series of even more original grounds (which are thus essential to the constitution of such figures as values).

While there are many such grounds, the kind that mediates sign-object relations is the most pressing for the arguments that follow (see figure 18). In particular, for agents to relate objects to signs requires that they have *sensibilities* to, and *assumptions* regarding: (1) the properties entities and events have; (2) the ways entities and events relate to each other through causalities and contiguities; (3) the conventions agents share for pointing to, and providing information about, entities and events (where such entities and events include themselves, each other, the collectivities they belong to, the world itself, and any other world they might care to imagine or be forced to reside in). Such sensibilities to, and assumptions about, qualitative, causal, and conventional relations—however real or imagined—allow such agents to make the connections that *drive semiotic processes*—which includes the play of consciousness. (Note, then, that Hume got here way before Peirce.) And such sensibilities and associations themselves usually *derive from semiotic processes*. Indeed, human semiotic agents are particularly good at figuring their own grounds through their semiotic processes—pointing out (and picking apart) their own and others' qualities, causalities, and conventions.

In regard to *conventions*, for example, there are a wide variety of relations on display in this story. First, and most obviously, there is the grammar and lexicon of Q'eqchi' (as a code, or set of relatively symbolic associations, that relates signs to objects, or signifiers to signifieds). We have already described some of the subtleties of such associations at length in our discussion of the Saussurean value (or Fregean sense) of various linguistic constructions in Q'eqchi'. Second,

---

Sign ⟶ Object

The *sensibilities* and *assumptions* semiotic agents have regarding the qualities, causalities, contiguities and conventions that exist in some world (and/or across multiple worlds), insofar as such sensibilities and assumptions allow such agents to relate otherwise disparate entities and events, including themselves and other agents, as signs to objects.

(Think Hume on habit, Kant on the aprioris of reason, and anthropologists on culture.)

Figure 18. Semiotic Potentials

and *very* loosely speaking, there are the felicity conditions of Austinian speech acts (themselves the pragmatic generalization of the truth conditions discussed
in section 9), and discursive moves more generally.
relatively shared assumptions regarding what contexts
need to be in place for such actions to be appropriate,
and what contexts come to be in place if such actions
are effective. Indeed, as will be discussed at length in
later sections, the entire story turns on a ritual request
and offering, the man's unintended flouting of a felicity
condition (in particular, give without misgiving), and
the consequences thereof (in particular, a returned
offering, and hence an ultimately ineffective ritual).
While there are many other conventions on display, a
more important claim is that such relatively symbolic
associations also play a role in mediating the causal
and qualitative relations that will now be discussed—
thereby ensuring that many such relations, however
motivated as opposed to arbitrary they thereby are, or
at least seem to be, are nonetheless relatively collectiv-
ity-dependent and historically specific.

In regard to *causalities* and *contiguities*, there are
even more relations on display in this story. For example,
just as speech actions are subject to felicity conditions,
so too are physical actions, and techniques of the body
more generally: agents have assumptions regarding what
contexts need to be in place for such actions to be causally feasible, and what contexts come to be in place if
such actions are causally efficacious. What must one do,
and how much must the world respond, in order for such
actions to be *satisfied*, such that the world (more or less)
comes to resemble the plan or intention of the actor?
How does one journey to a temple, open a door, carry

a chain, deposit an offering, reach into one's pocket, make a sound, or utter a sentence? More generally, to simply act and exist in the world requires a huge set of relatively tacit assumptions and unconscious sensibilities regarding the causal ways of the world: available force fields, and their channeling of causes into effects, behaviors into results, instigations into sensations, experiences into affects and beliefs, affects and beliefs into habits and actions (not to mention symptoms and outbursts), and of course signs into interpretants. As we saw in section 4, during our discussion of inalienable possessions and personhood, there are partonomies on display: understandings of wholes and their parts, of social networks and their nodes, that license metonymic associations. Such partonomies not only structure person-part and collectivity-person relations, but also substance-quality and individual-substance relations, and so are part and parcel of human ontologies. For example, What kind of person is the man? What kind of divinity is the lord? What kind of metal is the chain? What kinds of people are the Q'eqchi'? And, more generally, What kinds of kinds are there for speakers of Q'eqchi'? Moreover, if an individual is understood to belong to a certain kind (such as male rather than female, gold rather than silver, native rather than foreign, cousin rather than sibling, or Mayan rather than Christian), what behaviors might we expect from them, and what dimensions (or qualities), in what degrees (or intensities), might be evinced by them?

In regard to such *qualities* and, in particular, the ways seemingly distinct entities may have qualities in common, the story precisely turns on a man's presumption that sighted eyes have a price, just like golden chains. As we saw in section 12, to even compare two entities, and thereby represent them as having different, or similar, degrees of a particular dimension, presumes they have the quality or dimension in question. While price is a particularly interesting dimension in that it seems to be a quality of all substances, at least "nowadays" (or so the man thought), other qualities are more narrowly shared: What has weight, color, or aroma? What qualities are available to our vision, as opposed to our touch? Or, to return to the concerns of section 7, recall our discussion of replacement (*eeqaj*): What shared qualities do men have that allow them to substitute for each other in labor pools? And what shared properties do an effigy and a person have such that the former can replace the latter in an illness cure? And recall our discussion of neologisms in section 6: What qualities do certain entities have that allow them to be talked about in nonautochthonous terms, using either *kaxlan* (chicken/foreign) or *ch'iich'* (machete/metallic)? Finally, speakers of Q'eqchi' not only predicate the qualities *sa* and *ra* (sweet and bitter, good and bad, pleasure and pain) of food, and situations more generally, they also predicate such qualities of hearts. Recall from section 4 how happy or pleasureful (*sa*) the man's heart became when he was granted sight; imagine how sad or pained (*ra*) it must have become when his sight was taken away. Stanley Jeyaraja Tambiah's classic account of quality transference in magic rituals foregrounds similar facts. As does Nancy Munn's classic account of relatively domain-general, or substance-wide, qualities that are not prices per se, but nonetheless constitute values that are striven for. Indeed, for speakers of Q'eqchi', the nominalization of *sa* as *sahilal* (happiness, tastiness, goodness, contentment) constitutes an overarching value, often explicitly thematized, that they actively strive for. For example, and as will be further discussed in section 29, when the parts of a person (such as their eyes, and inalienable possessions more generally), and hence the person herself, flourish, the heart is *sa*, and the person is happy or content; and when the parts founder, the heart is *ra*, and the person is sad or depressed.

The point of focusing on such semiotic grounds, then, is not to identify sign-object relations as relatively iconic, indexical, or symbolic (nor to chastise those who only focus on the symbolic, while ignoring the iconic and the indexical). Rather, the point is to focus on this ensemble of sensibilities and assumptions per se; and its specification, transformation, and conditions of possibility. In particular, to even call a semiotic process iconic, indexical, or symbolic presupposes that we know something about the qualities, causal contiguities, and conventions orienting the semiotic agents so engaged. And, insofar as different agents and collectivities of agents have different sensibilities and assumptions as to possible qualities, causes, and conventions, their *semiotic potentials*—that is, their capacities and propensities to engage in particular semiotic processes—are different. Indeed, *such semiotic potentials are to semiotic processes what power is to its exercise*. And just as labor power is, in a Marxist tradition, an overarching value (so far as it is the source of all other values), such potentials should be, from a semiotic stance, overarching values: what we strive to analyze, understand, disclose, and perhaps even stoke or quell, through our scholarship.

Indeed, when such potentials are widely shared, and intersubjectively so, they constitute a large part of a collectivity's *semiotic commons*, traditionally known as "culture," itself a core building block in the constitution of possible worlds (not to mention a necessary resource for residing in some actual world). Tragically, but needless to say, such a commons is all too easily enclosed. The commodity you have in your hands, and scan with your eyes, being a case in point.

17. The Commodity Is a Semiotic Process

As diagrammed in figure 19, the commodity is a semiotic process. The sign component is a *use value*: three bushels of wheat, 8,000 cocoa beans, a golden chain, the telling of a story, the story itself (or a small book purporting to interpret it), the storyteller's verbal prowess (or semiotic potential), the translator's bilingual competence (or labor power), and so forth. The interpretant component is an *exchange value*: some other use value that could be exchanged for it, including a sum of money. And the object component is an *(economic) value*. For Marx, this would be something like the amount of socially necessary labor time incorporated in, or represented by, the use value and exchange value in question. But in other paradigms, other ontologies of the commodity, it could be otherwise. For example, it could be something like degree of desirability for the use value (and exchange value) in question, itself dependent on some collectivity and the agents within it (and hence their interests, imaginaries, social relations, senses of importance, semiotic grounds, or values more generally). Or it could turn on the amount of effort (qua work and energy) incorporated in the use value, and willing to be expended, or spent, by someone wishing to acquire it. Indeed, it probably involves features of all three of these frames, and much more besides.

Notice that all three components of the commodity (qua semiotic process) were values for Marx. There is value in use (UV): a certain quantity of some kind of substance or utility, itself capable of satisfying a desire directly, serving as a means to satisfy a desire, or producing something capable of satisfying a desire. There is value in exchange (EV): typically another value in use, and/or a symbolic token of value (qua money, credit, and/or a promise to pay). And, at least in Marx, there is value per se (V): some third entity, however real, abstract, or intersubjective, that both the use value and exchange value stand in relation to.

To be sure, this third component is often understood to be the most important, or valuable, of the three components (as values). But that said, from a semiotic stance, the overarching semiotic value (or meaning) of a semiotic process lies in the relation between relations that mediates these three components. That is to say, the semiotic value of a commodity is constituted by the relation among the components (in particular, the relation between the UV-V relation and the EV-V relation, not to mention the semiotic potentials that mediate such relations), not by any one of the components per se. And

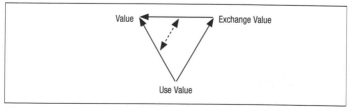

Figure 19. The Commodity as Semiotic Process

so use values, exchange values, and (economic) values not only have semiotic values embedded in them (for example, the use value component of a commodity can itself be a sign, semiotic process, or semiotic potential), they are themselves embedded in semiotic values (see figure 20). Phrased another way, commodities are inherently metasemiotic processes: consisting of a larger (embedding) semiotic process, each of whose components may be smaller (embedded) semiotic processes.

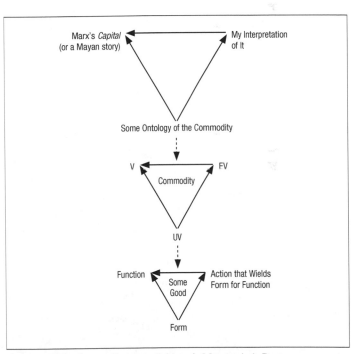

Figure 20. The Commodity as an Inherently Metasemiotic Process

18. Grounding Economic Value and/or Regimenting Price

Viewing the commodity from such a semiotic stance motivates the fact that there are three key categories in Marx's system (rather than two): use value, value, and exchange value. And it thereby motivates the fact that there are three key processes underlying any economy (at least in Marx's imaginary): consumption (oriented toward use value); production (oriented toward value); and circulation or exchange (oriented toward exchange value).

Phrased another way, and to return to our discussion of regimentation from sections 14 and 15, each component of the commodity plays a crucial role in the mediation of (economic) value. The value of a use value, for example, is dependent on the use value per se: as an instrument, it must serve a function that is deemed desirable or necessary by those who would wield it. And the value of a use value is dependent on its exchange value: What use values would others be willing to sacrifice for it, in what proportions? Crucially as well, the value of any use value is dependent on the relation between supply and demand. For example, if many people desire or need the use value in question, but few were actually produced during the last business cycle (or available around here), then the exchange values others would give for that use value will increase. Finally, the value of a use value is iconic-indexically related to the labor that produced that use value: indexical because causally realized; iconic because proportionally incorporated. And the value of any particular use value is also iconic-index-ically related to the labor that produced all other use values on the market: indexical because in any statistical ensemble each part is related to every other part of the whole; iconic because inversely proportional as part is to whole. Marx seemed to be acutely aware of these facts (and many others besides), and of the role they played in the mediation of (economic) value. It should be emphasized, then, that even Marx didn't really advocate a "labor theory of value." Rather, he offered a *production-circulation-consumption theory of value*, one that made principled reference to all three components of the commodity (qua semiotic process), and their interrelations.

This mediation of value by production, circulation, and consumption may be seen in figure 21. In this way, the value of a commodity, as will be ultimately expressed in, or at least proportional to, its price-form, is just as dependent on "supply and demand" (qua circulation) and "desire and need" (qua consumption) as it is on means of production and labor power (qua production). And, depending on the commodity at issue, and the timescale of interest, any one of these factors may be more or less determining of value (and/or price).

Similar facts also apply to the metaphysics of commodities, and to ontologies of goods more generally. As will start to be shown in section 25, when we discuss agency and personhood, while it is easy to fixate on an essence/appearance distinction—say, body versus mind, factory versus market, power versus its exercise, subject versus predicate, substance versus quality, invisible versus visible, money versus coin, and even hearts versus eyes—that is itself a superficial distinction. A more robust account of power, action, and value necessarily has three (recursively reticulated) components (and not just self-embedding binary oppositions).

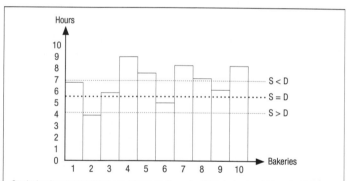

Graph showing amount of time (y-axis) required by each of 10 bakeries (x-axis) to make 100 loaves of bread. The average time necessary to make 100 loaves of bread is therefore 5.5 hours (shown by the heavy, dotted line). If 1 hour = $100, then each loaf of bread should have the value of 550 cents. Assuming that there are 1,000 families buying one loaf of bread per day, then supply is equal to demand (S = D), and a loaf of bread does indeed cost $5.50. However, if the number of families grows, then supply may be less than demand (S < D); and if the number of families shrinks, then supply may be greater than demand (S > D). Moreover, demand itself is grounded in the desires and needs of a buying public, which itself can change irrespective of the fluctuating size of this public: via taste, fashion, holiday baking, a craze for sandwiches, and so forth. In such cases, it is as if each of the bakeries—and hence all bakeries—were working more or less than socially necessary, and hence the price their bread will realize when sold either grows or shrinks (at least in Marx's ontology of the commodity).

Figure 21. Production-Circulation-Consumption Theory of Value

19. A Mayan Ontology of the Anticommodity

We have just outlined some key features of the commodity form as a semiotic process. Having gone through all that, we should stress that the man's giving of a golden chain, and the god's healing of the man's eyes, while definitely a semiotic process (the offering relating to the healing as sign to interpretant), is almost certainly not an instance of commodity exchange. (Recall our discussion of singularities, replacements, and commodities in section 7.) Indeed, it was only when the man had his misgivings and evaluated the relative worth of eyes and chains, and hence treated the exchange as if it were similar to a commodity exchange (in one widespread framing), that the god refused the offering.

In some sense, Lord Chajul seemed to be sensitive to the fact that eyes aren't really made like chains. While they might be radically valuable—indeed priceless—like inalienable possessions more generally, they did not have economic value, were not the effects of labor, and/or had no obvious price. Moreover, one good was alien (referred to with a Spanish loan word); the other was radically inalienable, local, and intimate—literally, a part of a person. The second reason is that the exchangers themselves were not equal in status: if two agents, radically dissimilar in their respective powers, exchange goods, one can hardly expect the goods to be commensurate. Recall our discussion of redistribution (and reciprocation) in section 2. The third reason is that the value of the action did not adhere in *what* was given (the gold chain), but rather in *the way* it was given.

Giving in such a way, or mode, that an internal state, or affective relation, holds: giving with all one's heart, and thus giving without calculation or misgivings. In short, and looking ahead to section 30, not exchanging in such a way that the exchange maximized profit, or minimized cost, as instrumental values; but rather exchanging in such a way that the act of giving conformed to an ethical standard, or existential value.

In some sense, then, the story expressed a local theory of commodity exchange insofar as it made explicit an alternative mode of exchange: one turning on offerings, inalienable possessions, and noncalculative intentions. And it used this to make explicit a particular moral value, or ethical standard: don't behave in the temple as you do in the market. In some sense, it offered a Mayan ontology of the anticommodity.

Somewhat ironically, it takes a fetish object (Lord Chajul, qua invisible god) to make explicit a fetish object (the golden chain, qua flashy good). Looking ahead to the next two sections, as different as such goods and gods are in kind, both are parasites in fact: while the latter misdirects our desires, the former intercepts our thoughts. To be sure, for many hardcore Marxists, it also takes a fetish object—Marx's collected writings—to make explicit a fetish object: the commodity fetish per se. Indeed, if their own writings are any indication, many of them are deeply committed to a *belabor* theory of value. (So I myself will try not to say too much more about the fetish until section 33.)

20. Energy, Work, and Friction

While a labor theory of value is not really central to this story, the value of work and energy (in a physicist's sense) certainly is. As may be seen in figure 22, there is an uncanny resemblance between Marx's account of commodity production and Claude Shannon's account of message communication (which itself underlay Jakobson's account of the speech event, and hence the poetic analysis of Saussurean equivalence classes undertaken in earlier sections). For Marx, a sum of money (M) is converted into a commodity (C), which is then subject to a production process (P), resulting in another commodity (C′), which is converted back into a sum of money (M′). For Shannon, a message (M) is converted into a signal (S), which is then subject to interference by noise (N), resulting in another signal (S′), which is converted back into a message (M′). For both theorists the conversions in question retain a third term (shown by slightly thinner lines in the diagrams). In particular, for Marx a transaction in the market (either M-C or C′-M′) more or less preserves value. For Shannon, a translation by a code (either M-S or S′-M′) more or less preserves meaning. For Marx, production is of a different order than transaction: it causes an ordering of matter, and the creation of value. For Shannon, noise is of a different order than translation: it causes a disordering of signal, and the loss of meaning. For Marx, the desired goal of capitalism is an effect that is different from the original cause: not so much a new commodity as a larger sum of money (and so more value). In a word, *profit*. For Shannon, the desired goal of communication is an effect that is identical to the original cause: the same signal, and hence the same message (and so the same meaning). In a word, *fidelity*. In short, for both theorists there are three terms (money, commodity, value; message, signal, meaning) and two orders (transaction versus production; translation versus destruction).

Marx and Shannon were similar in another way: both were radically dependent on, and yet at one degree of remove from, a thermodynamic imaginary (or reality). To see how, imagine a canonical physical system like a pendulum (or a child on a swing). Over time, such a system follows a particular path through its configuration space: at any moment of time, it has a certain position and momentum; and across moments of time, it has different positions and different momenta. Crucially, assuming no work is done on the system (or

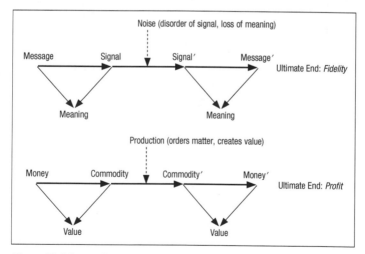

Figure 22. Message Communication (Shannon) and Commodity Production (Marx)

by the system), and assuming there are no dissipating forces (such as friction), then a quintessential value is preserved across distinct configurations of the system: *energy*. Conservation laws in physics, themselves turning on underlying symmetries of dynamical systems, are the prototypical modes of equivalence. However, if the system is subject to work or friction, then such an energetic value is gained or lost across distinct configurations of the system. In short, if Marx focused on the role of work (qua "labor") in creating value, Shannon focused on the role of friction (qua "noise") in destroying meaning. Both authors, like many physicists before them, focused on the tension between relatively reversible and irreversible processes, as well their conditions and consequences.

21. Conversion, Preservation, and Evil

So how does all that relate to gold chains and Lord Chajul? Firstly, it should be remembered that the two processes just described enchain with each other (and embed in each other) indefinitely. For example, by the time you are reading this essay, the story in question has been through many processes of the Shannon sort; and so it has been converted across many material orders along the way. To name just a few, it has gone from internal speech to external speech, the firing of neurons to the vibrations of vocal cords; from vibrating vocal cords to undulating sound waves; from sound waves to oscillating ear drums (or perhaps a recording); from ear drums, back through brains, to the movements of pencils or the clacking of keys; from handwriting to typewriting; from document to mimeograph; from mimeograph to typesetting; from typesetting to published books (themselves conveyed from factories to libraries); from published books, through scanned copy, to PDF (qua portable document format), itself saved as a bit string on a server somewhere, to be subsequently downloaded by me … (And, note, we haven't even touched its "translation" and "circulation" proper—from Q'eqchi' to Spanish or English; from another Mayan language (perhaps Ixil)—or perhaps even a sermon in Spanish—to Q'eqchi'. For this story, surely, has been 'around'.)

Crucially, the story was also buffeted by lots of noise along the way. How much of what was remembered was said; how much of what was said was heard; how much of what was heard was written; how much of what was handwritten was typewritten? And so on, both down and up the line. In what state, with what mistakes? In particular, there would probably be far less fidelity, due to the disorganizing nature of noise, had not many actors labored to conserve it. In the real world, not just creating value, but simply preserving it (in the face of noise, and of entropic processes more generally), takes effort. Indeed, putting Marx and Shannon together, we might go so far as to reframe (concrete) labor, or value-producing action, as follows: it does not just give form to substance for the sake of function; it does not just organize complexity for the sake of predictability; and it does not just preserve form to retain function; it also involves caring for messages in order to preserve their meaning (or information) and protecting signals in order to safeguard their content (or correlates).

Indeed, in this Marx-Shannon imaginary, one doesn't just have to protect a message from noise (that which interferes); one also has to protect it from enemies (that which intercepts). If noise stops a pattern from propagating to the "right" place (a friend), enemies cause a pattern to propagate to the "wrong" place (a foe). Indeed, among cybersecurity experts this *third* term (which stands orthogonal to the relation between source and destination, or signer and interpreter) often goes by the name of Eve, reminiscent of she who (was said to have) caused the fall of man (by learning a secret she wasn't privy to), by accepting messages from Evil itself (the serpent).

(To be sure, this third term (qua enemy, parasite, or noise) doesn't have to be evil incarnate, and the source and destination don't have to be constituted by different agents. As we saw above, when the man spoke to himself, or inside his heart, his words must have been heard, or intercepted, by Lord Chajul. Indeed, in a Marxist imaginary, capitalists are the quintessential parasite: they don't just own the means of production; they also stand orthogonal to every transaction insofar as they intercept the surplus before it can return to the hands of its source. Figure 23 shows an even wider range of possible roles for this third term, highlighting its relatively ambiguous valence, as well as its relation to Peirce's notion of thirdness, not to mention the whole of actor-network theory.)

All this puts us directly in the realm of (one particularly famous story's account of) good and evil, and morality more generally (not to mention gender and genesis). To be sure, this other story, unlike the story told here, was not only converted (retained, translated, interpreted, and cared for, across many orders, with many branches, with as much variation as invariance); it was also used to convert.

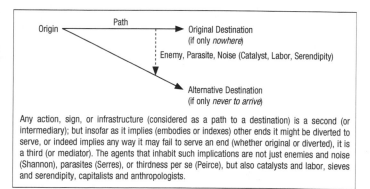

Figure 23. Enemies, Parasites, Noise; Catalysts, Labor, and Serendipity

Apropos of evil, and conversion proper, it should thus be mentioned that the story analyzed here was originally published in an edited volume sponsored by the Summer Institute for Linguistics (SIL), once described as "a faith-based nonprofit organization committed to serving language communities worldwide as they build capacity for sustainable language development." In particular, it was one of eleven stories collected from native speakers of Q'eqchi', a set constituting the content of one chapter of an edited volume called *According to Our Ancestors: Folk Texts from Guatemala and Honduras.*[9] Members of SIL, working with unnamed speakers of some fifteen indigenous languages, undertook the labor of "collecting" the stories (inciting and recording their retelling, not to mention extracting their values from context, and thereby enclosing them as "texts"), translating them into English, and analyzing and interpreting their collective meaning. For example, a lengthy introduction discusses recurrent tropes and motifs, areal connections, typical moral dilemmas, types of animal figures, and so forth. It was precisely a PDF version of this volume, that I found online and downloaded, that became the starting point for this essay. In sending their volume out to a public of potential addressees it is not clear whether members of SIL (qua message source) would consider an anthropologist to be an intended recipient (qua message destination), or an intercepting Eve along the way.

That said, note the way that this organization flags its nonprofit status in its self-description, loudly proclaiming that the institution is outside of Marx's description of a capitalist circuit: M' is not supposed to be larger than M. (And, indeed, I paid no money for my PDF. It was a use value without an exchange value.) I presume that, rather than profit, the value this organization strives for is—at least in part—fidelity of beliefs (in divine words) qua faith. Indeed, their collecting and curating of indigenous stories, itself part of a larger project of documenting native languages, went hand in hand with their larger project of getting "the good word" out. That is to say, *the good as demanded by God*. This is a very different kind of conversion: not money to commodity (preserving value), or message to signal (preserving meaning); rather, the people stay more or less the same (as vessels), while their values change. Interestingly, their Saussurean values were also meant to stay the same (recall SIL's stated commitment to serving language communities, and to preserving indigenous languages more generally); it is only their existential values (and cosmological beliefs, I presume, qua commitment to particular truth values) that were meant to change. SIL, then, uses *their* words to bring them "the word."

22. Affordances, Instruments, and Actions

While we have so far focused on semiotic processes that are stereotypically discursive and economic, it should be stressed that semiosis is far more general (see figure 24). An *affordance* is a semiotic process: the sign is a (relatively and/or prototypically) natural feature; the object is the purchase provided by that feature (whatever it enables or constrains a particular creature from doing in a particular context); and a key interpretant is an instrument that incorporates that feature (or an action that heeds that feature) so far as it provides purchase. For example, just as iron might be made into a machete (given its hardness), gold might be made into a chain (given its luster). Insofar as such substances have certain dimensions in specific degrees, and insofar as such dimensions and degrees are consequential to the sensations and instigations of agents, they permit or prohibit those agents from undertaking certain actions, including actions that produce instruments.

An *instrument* is a semiotic process: the sign is some (relatively and/or prototypically) artificed entity; the object is the function served by such a form; and one key interpretant is an action that wields such a form for the sake of its function. For example, a golden chain might be worn as a sign of status, given as an offering,

Semiotic Process	Sign	Object	Some Possible Interpretants
Affordance	Natural feature	Purchase	Incorporating instrument, heeding action, etc.
Instrument	Artificed entity	Function	Wielding action, created instrument, etc.
Action	Controlled behavior	Purpose	Another's reaction, representing utterance, etc.

Figure 24. Affordances, Instruments, and Actions as Semiotic Processes (qua Ideal Types)

stored as a source of value, loaned to secure an alliance, hidden as a target of thieves, sold in return for a price, or melted down to be transformed into something else entirely. As we saw in section 17, the use value component of a commodity is typically an instrument (in a specific quantity), and hence an embedded semiotic process: a bolt of cloth, a bushel of wheat, a *xiikil* of cocoa beans, a book of Mayan stories.

And an *action* is a semiotic process: the sign is a (relatively and/or prototypically) controlled behavior; the object is the purpose of that behavior; and one key interpretant is another's reaction to that behavior (so far as it is directed toward, or designed to fulfill, such a purpose), including a disruption of that behavior or a description of that behavior. What was the man doing in the temple? He was offering his golden chain to a god, in order that his eyes be healed. Why did you tell me this story? To teach you to give with all your heart.

Note, then, that such purchases, functions, and purposes are values in our original sense: signs stand for them; and agents strive for them (or at least with them). Note that any natural feature, artificed entity, or controlled behavior may have many such values projected onto it—depending on the heeding, wielding, and representing practices of an interpreting agent (see figure 25). But that said, such value-mediating interpretants cannot range too far insofar as they are regimented, or sanctioned: not just by human and nonhuman agents, but also by the very signs they are interpreting, and the objects (understood as objections) that those signs stand for. Indeed, the semiotic grounds mediating such sign-object relations are usually highly motivated (or iconic-indexical), insofar as their form (qua sign) is so tightly coupled to their function (qua object). Note, then, in a tradition most forcefully articulated by Marshall Sahlins, that "utility" (or practical reason) is not to be contrasted with "meaning." Rather, it is just one species of semiosis among many others—special perhaps only insofar as it often seems so highly motivated and forcibly regimented.

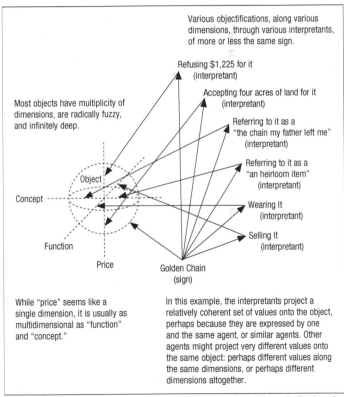

Figure 25. Some Possible Interpretants of a Sign (and an Object So Projected)

23. Action, Agency, Excellence, and Existential Values

Action, needless to say, is central to value in multiple ways. As we just saw, actions are oriented to values (as goals or ends). And actions depend on values (as means or tools): not only do our actions heed affordances and wield instruments, they require infrastructures and institutions for their effects. As Marx and others argued at length, actions produce value (as outcomes or effects, such as instruments and commodities more generally, often proportional to the time or effort that went into undertaking them). And, as this story shows, actions—and, in particular, discursive actions—disclose and enclose value: what is valuable; why it is valuable; how can it be obtained, protected, inculcated, captured, or transformed. Indeed, just what was one important purpose underlying the recounting of this story, if not to figure and frame, and thus disclose and enclose, the distinction between false values (or idols) and real ones, as well as the repercussions of mistaking one for the other?

Action is central to agency. Insofar as we (more or less) control when and where a behavior is undertaken, compose what behavior is undertaken (or what purpose it points to, or is meant to satisfy), and commit to (or anticipate) what effect such a behavior will have (including how it will be interpreted by others), we are often held accountable for it, and thereby regimented because of it, if only through inference or innuendo: subject to reward or punishment, praise or blame, pleasure or pain, success or failure, pride or shame. And we are not just held accountable for the effect of the behavior (what happened because of what we did); we are also held accountable for the values that led to that behavior (why we did what we did). What did the man do—if only as a private calculative action, itself oriented to a false idol (price)—that caused the god to return his offering and take back his gift?

Finally, actions are not just indicative of character (the actions we undertake often determine the kind of person we are, as part to whole, or effect to cause), they also constitute who we are. In carrying out certain actions, in specific ways, according to standards of excellence, or conditions of felicity, we literally build character or accrue virtue. (At least according to the ethics of Aristotle, the Catholic tradition influenced by Aristotle, and a certain moment in Q'eqchi'-Maya culture, itself likely influenced by that tradition, however marginally, mistakenly, or ill-advisedly.) When giving, if you seek to do good, or be excellent, and thereby exhibit and/or acquire a very high degree of a virtuous or goodly dimension, *give with all your heart.*

With the foregoing ideas in mind, the next several sections will focus on what might best be termed *existential values* (in a variety of guises or frames). Section 24 will focus on ultimate ends, or relatively high-order purposes underlying long-term actions. Sections 25–28 will focus on performative ends, or the exercising of present powers as a means to gather future and/or further powers, specifically through economic transactions and other ritual processes. Section 29 will relate such issues to our discussion of inalienable possessions, focusing on relatively reflexive ends—in particular, all the auto-technic and auto-telic actions underlying an agent's care of itself. And section 30 will focus on the evaluative standards that allow us to choose among possible actions.

As will be shown, such existential values are often understood to be the most valuable of values: felicity, summum bonum, an end in itself, the good life, human flourishing, prosperity, a happy heart. Indeed, given the antagonist of our story, it is not without significance that Aristotle's word for the highest end, *eudaemonia*, often translated as "felicity," is composed of the Saussurean values, or signs, *eu* (good/true/genuine) and *daemon* (spirit).

24. From Short-Term to Long-Term Action

The opening lines of the story showcase some general characteristics of action—at least as it is understood by speakers of Q'eqchi'. A man has an overarching desire, or goal: to be able to see. There is an overarching means for achieving this goal, if only implicitly formulated as a plan or intention: make a pilgrimage to a god who is known to work miracles, such that the god might heal his eyes. There is a sequence of actions in a means-ends chain, such that prior actions in the chain serve as conditions of possibility for later actions: he went to the temple; when he got there, he entered the temple; when he was in the temple, he went to the altar; when he got to the altar, he requested that his eyes be healed and gave the golden chain as an offering. The final end of this sequence of actions is the achievement of the overarching goal, the realization of the initial plan, or the satisfaction of the underlying intention: the god will (hopefully, possibly) accept the offering, agree to the request, and heal the man's eyes in return.

To be sure, as the story progresses, there is a reformulation of the plan along the way. In particular, the man wonders whether, and indeed calculates how, a different path might have led to the same destination (whether and how he might have given less to get the same return). And it is precisely this speculative action that leads to the parasitic thwarting of the plan, and the nonrealization of the purpose—precisely through the flouting of the felicity conditions of an offering, at least in the eyes of Lord Chajul, himself an agent of both transmutation (gold to sight) and regimentation (misgiving to blindness). Finally, in this thwarting of his purpose, or upending of his plan, the man comes to realize there is an even higher good (than getting his sight): giving with all his heart (at least when dealing with gods). An ethical insight, rather than an economic good (or physical sight per se) becomes the overarching value, or higher purpose, toward which, the man learns, he should subsequently strive.

25. Agency, Personhood, Power

Just as affordances, instruments, and actions may be framed as semiotic processes, so too may a person, actor, or agent more generally (see figure 26). The object component is a mode of power: a status, kind, substance, competence, potential, or identity. The sign component is an exercise of that power: a role, index, quality, performance, or action. And the interpretant component is another agent's way of relating to that power (that comes into being through its exercise): a speech act or mental state, an affective unfolding or mood, an action or habit, a change in footing or attitude, a semiotic process or potential, a tribute or wage, a gift or commodity, a way of recognizing or regimenting, and even another mode of power.

As this story shows, many exercises of power are relatively contingent, causal processes: Lord Chajul, a quintessential agent, will often produce a miracle if made an acceptable offering. This power is recognized by the man: perhaps he has witnessed past exercises of such a power; perhaps he has only heard reports of them; but, in any case, in setting out to the temple, he expects, or at least hopes for, further exercises of such a

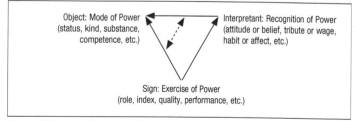

Object: Mode of Power
(status, kind, substance, competence, etc.)

Interpretant: Recognition of Power
(attitude or belief, tribute or wage, habit or affect, etc.)

Sign: Exercise of Power
(role, index, quality, performance, etc.)

Figure 26. Agent, Power, or Person as Semiotic Process

power from that agent. And the power itself is relatively open-ended: so long as one gives the offering with all one's heart, and thus without calculation or misgiving, what is requested will be granted. In this case, it is sight itself; for other people, making other offerings, it could be otherwise. And, just as Lord Chajul is such an agent in the world of the blind man (understood as something like his ontology, imaginary, cosmology, culture, or context), *Dios* or "God" is a more or less equivalent agent in the world of the nameless narrator.

In a tradition that originates with Aristotle, the chain offered by the man to Lord Chajul is also such an agent, understood as a primary substance, or concrete individual. Being-gold per se would be its most important underlying power, understood as a secondary substance, or kind. The qualities that such a substance has would be exercises of its power—for example, its color, density, or ductility (perhaps best understood not just as dimension-in-sufficient-degrees, but also in *if-then* terms). For example, it appears yellow when examined in sunlight; sinks when placed in water; melts in fire; is malleable when bit; and (perhaps even) returns a high price if sold. And the man himself might come to recognize that the chain is indeed made of gold through some of its qualities, and thereby expect it to exhibit other qualities that would be in keeping with it being-gold. (Assuming, of course, he is beholden to such an ontology, resides in such a world, inhabits a certain culture, possesses a certain semiotic potential, or is committed to such a system of categories.)

To be sure, in his interaction with Lord Chajul, and in his offering of the golden chain, the man also comes to change his categories, update his imaginary, transform his ontology, and reworld (in part by "rewording") the world he resides in. In particular, he learns that the god will only exercise his power if certain conditions are met: what matters is not the offering per se, but rather the way the offering is made. Concomitantly, he learns that the price of the golden chain, its expensiveness per se, is not an essential quality of an offering; but that, rather, the state of the heart of the one making the offering is. As we saw, the god did not exercise a power that the man expected; in part, because the chain did not have the quality that the man presumed; or, rather, while the chain did have that quality, it was ancillary to the performative efficacy of the offering by which the man called upon, or enlisted, the god's power. And, indeed, the insight the blind man ultimately acquires is precisely a hard-earned recognition of the essential powers (traits or states) of golden chains, possessed hearts, and Lord Chajul. Or, if you like, the key dimensions, and sufficient degrees, of gods, goods, and "the good."

26. Credit, Debt, Ownership, and the Personification of Deontic Modality

Another way of framing similar dynamics comes from crossing Ralph Linton with George Herbert Mead. A status is a collection of rights and responsibilities; a role is an enactment of that status (actually acting on such a right, or according to such a responsibility); and an attitude is a relation to a status through a role. In this framing, a canonical semiotic process, itself a key component of any social relation (in formation), is as follows: I perceive your role (qua sign); I infer your status (qua object); and I come to expect (qua interpretant) other roles that would be in keeping with your status (so long as I have a particular semiotic potential, am committed to a certain ontology, or was habituated in a certain culture). To return to the concerns of sections 3 and 4: if a status is deontic modality personified (permission and obligation), a role is personhood actualized, and an attitude is such a persona internalized (see figure 27).

Such statuses, qua modes of permission and obligation, are legion. From Mauss, in the context of gift giving, we get at least three: the obligation to give,

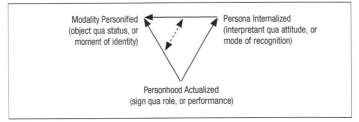

Figure 27. Deontic Modality and Personhood

accept, and reciprocate. From Innes, in the context of creditors giving commodities to debtors in exchange for money (understood as credit), we get at least four: the right the creditor acquires to payment (qua satisfaction of the credit); the obligation the debtor acquires to pay the debt; the right of the debtor to release himself from debt by tender of an equivalent debt (typically another credit); and the obligation of the creditor to accept this tender in satisfaction of the credit. As I saw it, "Facticity ... as a combination of the cultural relativism of [Franz] Boas and the social fact of [Émile] Durkheim ... is best understood as a kind of second-order modality: deontic pairings of types of behaviors and types of circumstances that *must be this way* (here, now, and among us), but *may be otherwise* (there, then, and among them)."[10]

To return to Marx, note that exchange value, as embodied in money, may often be best understood as the quantification and abstraction of right (or responsibility). It is abstract because what one has rights to is not specified, being any use value that has a certain exchange value. And it is quantified because the exchange value fixes the relative proportion of rights that one has access to. For example, my \$10 is abstract insofar as it is a right to any use value that has that exchange value (a particular quantity). And it is quantified, insofar as I have ten times as much right as someone who only has \$1. More generally, credit and debt may be framed as quantified and abstracted rights and responsibilities, respectively. Perhaps the real power of money, then, is in its contribution to, and quantitative reconfiguring of, deontic modality (which is, arguably, at least as old as humanity).

In this framing, to really own a specific commodity, or possess an amount of money, requires that one not just have a property status per se (for example the right to consume, use, or exchange the item in question). One must also provide evidence for, or offer signs of, such rights and responsibilities (not just deeds, receipts, and keys, but also physical possession of the item in question, as well as the performance of acts of acquisition, ownership, and use, not to mention metonymy, inalienability, sheer proximity, and physical incorporation). And such a property status, through such possessive roles, must be recognized by a range of other agents (in their beliefs and practices, habits and memories, institutions and imaginaries), however large or small in size, far or near in space-time, strong or weak in their recognition, severe or lax in their regimentation.

27. Felicity and Felicitousness, Aristotle and Austin

As Mead saw it, insofar as we act (qua sign) in relation to an ensemble of already existing attitudes (qua interpretants) as to our status or power (qua object), we are in the realm of the *me* (qua relative constraint); but insofar as our acts change such an ensemble of modes of recognition (as to our powers), we are in the realm of the *I* (or relative freedom). In some sense, the *me* is the self as *retended* by its past interactions and social relations; whereas the *I* is the self as *protending* of its future interactions and social relations. And just as every person, or interactant more generally, faces in two directions as once, so does every action and, in particular, every interaction or transaction. As may be seen in figure 28, then, in such a framing the self sits somewhere at—or around—the interface of two semiotic processes, and so is distributed as much as incipient (or latent), and hence only exists

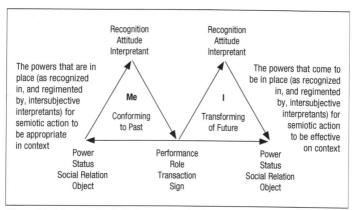

Figure 28. Mead on Symbolic Interaction (and Austin on Speech Acts)

as an intersubject and an interimsubject. As may also be seen, Mead got to a theory of performativity before J. L. Austin. (To be sure, Hobbes and Henry James Sumner Maine were there long before either of them.)

Crucially, in describing an offering gone awry, the story in question precisely shows some of the core felicity conditions of ritual acts, or symbolic interaction (which are themselves the pragmatic generalization of the satisfaction conditions underlying semantic regimentation, or truth value, that we saw in section 9). In particular, the offering will only be *appropriate* in context if the person does not just give something to the god (at the right temple, in the right way, through saying the right words, and so forth), but gives it with all their heart; and the offering will only be *effective* on context if the god in question does not just receive the offering, but also gives something in return (whose value is potentially incommensurate with the offering in question, as befits the relative statuses of people and gods). That is to say, the story itself is making intersubjectively known—to all members of the collectivity in which it circulates—the felicity conditions, qua conventional requirements, of a certain kind of ritual action. As the man comes to realize (bring into being, and become aware of) the felicity conditions of offerings through the repercussions of his infelicitous offering, we come to realize them through the story's portrayal of his realization, and hence at one or more degrees (or worlds) of remove from such repercussions.

For, as Austin so incisively noted, a key (meta-) felicity condition for any ritual action (or economic transaction) *qua eventive token* is that participants are in (relatively) intersubjective agreement as to the felicity conditions of such an action *qua conventional type*. A core function of such a story, then, is to help conventionalize such satisfaction conditions: to make them more widely known, intersubjectively recognized, and/or mutually regimented, by some collectivity (however open-ended, and hence *open to interpretation*, they might actually be—given all the latent and labile semiotic potentials underlying any such semiotic process).

Crucially, Austin's felicity conditions (qua conditions and consequences of properly satisfied actions) are themselves essential to Aristotle's notion of felicity (qua ultimate ends of all human action). In particular, by spelling out felicity conditions this story attempts to bring about a state of felicity—itself the highest of goods in Aristotle's ontology. Or, inverting the emphasis, as the story itself does, we see the relation between infelicitous actions and unhappy agents (and hence between error and affect more generally).

28. The *Hau*, qua Performativity and Inter(im) subjectivity of Economic Rituals

We have just seen one relatively ritualistic way a god might come to acquire a golden chain, and a man might come to acquire sighted eyes. Most transactions nowadays, at least in a widespread legal imaginary and commodity ontology, are more banal. So long as I (am recognized to) have rights to the commodity I intend to sell, and you (are recognized to) have rights to the money (perhaps best understood as credit, following Innes) you use to buy it; so long as we both freely agree to swap them in certain proportions (and so on and so forth); and so long as we do indeed swap them; then I come to be recognized as having rights to the money, and you come to be recognized as having rights to the commodity. (Contrast the forced transactions underlying the exchange of iron axes for *xiikils* of cocoa beans discussed in section 13.)

Crucially, to turn from Mead to Austin, both the modes of recognition that had to be in place for the transaction to be "appropriate" and the modes of recognition that come to be in place insofar as the transaction was "effective" are relatively inter-subjective. Loosely speaking, we both recognize that we each recognize the appropriate and effective statuses in question such that, in effect, we become a single, distributed, self-regimenting unit of account-ability in regard to the rights and responsibilities at issue (at least during the interim in question). More crucially still, insofar as it is all too easy for a relatively small self-regimenting unit of accountability to go awry, others—if not entire collectivities—are often enlisted or imposed to help regiment the modes of mutual recognition, qua inter(im)subjectively held, and socially distributed, interpretants. While Mead called this inter(im)subject the generalized other, and thought about it in terms of baseball (itself the most modal, or "other-wordly," of games), nowadays it is most clearly instantiated in the blockchains of Bitcoins and other cyptocurrencies.

Note, then, how radically distributed, and this-worldly, (this interpretation of) the *hau* actually is. In part, it consists of the statuses, qua obligations and permissions, of interactants (both before and after, and hence as roots and fruits of, their inter-action). In part, it consists of the semiotic processes and social relations of the actors involved, insofar as these evince and produce such statuses. And, in part, it consists of inter(im)subjectively held interpretants, qua modes of mutual recognition, that regiment such status-role, or power-exercise, relations. Note, then, that it is not just a space-time-person *manifold*; it is also its "manning" (qua personification) and "unfolding" (qua populating).

To be sure, just as the interactants themselves are typically persons, just as the things being exchanged often relate to those persons as effects to causes or parts to wholes, and just as the intersubjectively held interpretants are distributed across a population of people (if only as embedded in their infrastructures, embodied in their habits, encoded in their laws, or internalized in their imaginaries), it is easy to personify a small part of the entire process, and thereby set it apart, such that it might be fetishized as a god or sovereign (by some people, religion, or nation) or, worse yet, worshiped as a "mysterious force of compulsion" (by members of a long-standing academic tradition).

29. Renown and Resound: The Care of Self and the Curation of Stories

Let us return to our discussion of (in)alienable possessions and personhood from section 4 and offer yet another framing of existential value. Following the ideas of William James somewhat loosely, the self might be usefully understood as the ensemble of all that one may (or must) call one's own: for example, all of one's inalienable and alienable possessions; and so one's kith and kin, body parts and mental states, deeds and works, thoughts and opinions, house and lands, inherited and purchased goods, stocks and bonds, and so forth. Framed semiotically, and to slightly review, it consists of all our statuses (qua rights to, and responsibilities for, all the various possessions in question). It consists of our roles, qua status-producing and status-evincing actions (whatever we say or do that expresses our relation to such possessions, including simply having them). And it consists of others' attitudes toward such status-role relations (relatively intersubjective modes of recognition and regimentation in regard to such powers, and the ways we exercise and express them).

For James, sort of like for Spinoza before him, our desires are directed at either expanding the self, or staving off its contraction; and our affect (qua positive or negative moods and emotions) is itself the embodied register of the self's expansions and contractions. For speakers of Q'eqchi', one's desire, affect, and effort are also oriented toward caring for the self's contents and shoring up its contours. For example, striving to have one's blind eyes opened; or lamenting the unnecessary loss of a golden chain (when a cheaper possession might have done just as well); not to mention caring for one's family and fields, and tending to one's home and chickens. From such a vantage, one core sense of value—both instrumental and existential—turns on securing the regimenting attitudes of temporally, spatially, and socially distal others toward one's statuses (or powers) as evinced in and/or caused by the enactment of one's roles (or practices). Standing at the intersection of meaning and modality (via the Mead-Linton account of interaction), it is the ground of motivation (qua James's account of selfhood).

From this framing, one can see the radical entangling of three classic theories of value. Roughly speaking, Veblen's focus on pecuniary emulation (and theories of distinction more generally) foregrounded signs. Marx's focus on capitalist production, and on abstract labor time as the source of value, foregrounded objects (in the semiotic sense). And Malinowski's focus on circulation foregrounded interpretants. While all these components are, by necessity, interrelated by virtue of being part of a semiotic process, actions—and desires more generally—are often (mis-)directed at only a single component: (1) gaining greater and greater powers (qua objects or statuses); (2) expressing more and more emblematic performances (qua signs or roles); and (3) securing more and more widely distributed interpretants of such performance-power relations (qua interpretants or attitudes) (see figure 29).

As will be shown in the next three sections, what is true of selves is also true of stories—and, in particular, of stories about the virtuous actions of selves. They too are more or less powerful, or agentive, as a function of their distribution into space-time (and, more importantly, of their reworking of space-time), and hence of how deep and wide they "resound."

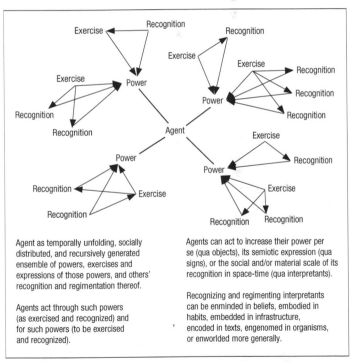

Agent as temporally unfolding, socially distributed, and recursively generated ensemble of powers, exercises and expressions of those powers, and others' recognition and regimentation thereof.

Agents act through such powers (as exercised and recognized) and for such powers (to be exercised and recognized).

Agents can act to increase their power per se (qua objects), its semiotic expression (qua signs), or the social and/or material scale of its recognition in space-time (qua interpretants).

Recognizing and regimenting interpretants can be enminded in beliefs, embodied in habits, embedded in infrastructure, encoded in texts, engenomed in organisms, or enworlded more generally.

Figure 29. Recursive Unfolding of Power, Exercise, and Recognition

30. Evaluative Standards, Ideals, and Second-Order Desire

Rather than frame value as an ultimate, performative, or reflexive end, as we have just been doing, we may also frame it as a higher-order desire, or evaluative standard. In such a framing, we have more ends than means, or more desires than resources, and so choices must be made. Value is thus understood not so much as a utility function but rather as an evaluative standard: a way to determine the relative desirability of different desires; or a way to evaluate the relative value of different values. Crucially, in order to choose (which course of action to undertake), one must be able to compare. And, in order to compare courses of action (or "goods" more generally), one usually requires that they be commensurate in some way. In particular, they should be relatively similar in regard to one or more desirable dimensions (if only preferability per se), however different they may be in regard to their degree of such dimensions. So long as they have the same quality, whatever its quantity, they may be ranked or compared, such that the agent in question can act accordingly.

As we saw in earlier sections, price (or economic value more generally) is one such dimension: it may be projected onto many different goods, and thereby used to make choices within and across a wide range of domains, via comparative practices. Recall section 12. And calculative action often depends on such choices. As most presciently foreseen by Aristotle, it does indeed seem to be the case that, just as price, or value in exchange, can be projected onto more and more domains, money per se (as that which meets price halfway) easily becomes the highest value. And, insofar as money is pure quantity (a dimension with no upper bound), and thus without limit, at least in Aristotle's ontology, it easily becomes a destructive value: not so much that which is valued above all other values, but that which is sought regardless of its devastating costs (to the polis and its people). In some sense, desires oriented toward it have no (finite) conditions of satisfaction. This story is, of course, a perfect example of the portrayal of such as costly calculation, and of its ultimate effects (however individualized, or inalienably possessed, and thus personified, they are), as well as the promulgation of a countervalue (through its aestheticization in a story, and its circulation through a telling).

When the underlying dimension used to determine preferability of options, or importance of actions, is something like price, and hence relatively monodimensional, domain-general, standardized, and quantitative, calculation is relatively easy (or so we are led to believe through the stories economists tell). And the rationality in question might be called *instrumental*, loosely following Max Weber's notion of means-rationality, or Charles Taylor's understanding of weak evaluation. There is a whole discipline devoted to understanding it; and a variety of counterdisciplines, or critical theories, often stemming from the disciples of Marx, devoted to explaining why that discipline misunderstands it. In contrast, when evaluation is relatively multidimensional, context-sensitive, nonstandardized, and qualitative (turning on gradable degrees, rather than measurable quantities), then the rationality in question might again be called *existential*, loosely following Weber's notion of ends-rationality, or Taylor's understanding of strong evaluation.

In situations governed by existential rationality (which probably include all situations), it may be argued that one weighs the relative desirability of different options, or the relative importance of possible actions, not by ranking them according to a single dimension like price, but by comparing their relative similarity to a set of prototypical, exemplary, or ideal actions, themselves undertaken by prototypical, exemplary, or ideal actors. Very loosely speaking, we assess the degree to which possible actions (options, destinations, or paths) are similar to prototypical, exemplary, or ideal actions, such that—in acting as such—we might come to be more like the actors in question (and thereby come to inhabit, if only by degrees, the kind of world they reside in) (see figure 30).

The actions that we strive to emulate (as exemplars or prototypes, ideals or ideal types) may be long: What is the entire life path of a righteous man, a humble person, an ethical subject, or a virtuous Mayan? Where do they seek to go, as it were, and how to they comport themselves to get there? Such paths may be short: What would a righteous person do when faced with some particular decision? How does a Mayan man make an offering with all his heart, or plant corn according to an honored tradition? Such paths may be exemplary: our sense of the life choices made by some particular, and particularly memorable, individual; someone we know, have heard about, and can "identify with." Such paths may be prototypical: a melding together in our minds, or an embodied arrangement in our habits, of the paths taken by different humble people, righteous men, or virtuous Maya. Depending on our current position in the world (as an origin), and our current purview (as to scale), we hold up different prototypes and exemplars to emulate, as ideals, and thereby determine which actions to undertake, what roles to perform, what identities to fulfill, and hence what values to strive for and, ultimately, what worlds to reside in.

To be sure, as this story shows, the prototypes, exemplars, or ideals we use as standards to determine our own actions may be inversions of the good, may be false gods, and thus show us how *not* to act, what

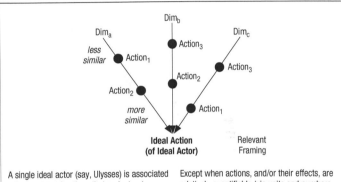

A single ideal actor (say, Ulysses) is associated with a variety of actions that project out a variety of dimensions: Should one be clever, impudent, dogged, or (relatively) faithful?

Comparing possible actions (1, 2, 3, etc.) as to their relative similarity to some ideal action (as carried out by an ideal actor) along various dimensions (a, b, c, etc.).

Except when actions, and/or their effects, are relatively quantifiable (via units and numbers, say), most dimensions are only by-degrees, or gradable (more or less), phenomena.

Not only the relevant dimensions (of the ideal action), but also the ideal action (most relevant for the choices in question), and possible actions (available for undertaking) are frame-dependent.

Stories (signs, etc.) project not only ideal actions, through their figuring of ideal actors, but also possible actions, relevant dimensions, and available framings.

Figure 30. Weighing Possible Actions Relative to Ideal Action

not to do, who *not* to be. So long as they are portable enough to pertain to "us," and the situations we find ourselves in, they may come to efficaciously work over, or existentially regiment, our actions, habits, affects, beliefs, dreams, and decisions.

As this story shows (and, indeed, instantiates), the figures and frames we use (and the ideal actions and actors we seek to emulate) spread and extend via social, semiotic, and material processes. Such figures and frames may be taken from relatively widespread anecdotes and stories, poems and myths; and they may be adopted from relatively narrow memories, or personal experiences. To study existential rationality is, in part, to study the *longue durée* genealogy and circulation of prototypes, exemplars, and ideals over history and across a population, as much as the real-time deployment and refinement of such figures (and grounds) by any contextually situated person, or collectivity of agents, in making an actual decision (even if only as imagined or narratively figured).

31. The Story as a Representation of Ideal Actions and/or Ethical Persons

This story provides precisely such an imaginary, example, ideal, or figure. It circulates—or rather is told, and retold, remembered and refashioned—in precisely such a way. And, quite reflexively, it portrays a real-time decision or action (of the man), and the flouting of certain felicity conditions, in order to govern real-time decisions and actions (of those who hear the story, internalize its values, and thereby seek to emulate them in practice).

Indeed, as the nameless narrator of the story indicates in her metacommentary, speakers of Q'eqchi' seem to have precisely such an understanding of the self-reflexive efficacy of such stories, with their figured ideals and personified values, for their own actions. And hence they seem to have an understanding of existential value that is comparable with this one—itself a combination of Weber's notion of ends-rationality and ideal types. For example, as seen in the first line of the following metacommentary (which corresponds to the last three sentences of the published text), right before the narrator characterizes the moral of the story as applying to "us," in our relationship to "God" (Spanish *Dios*), he or she refers to the story itself using the Spanish word *ejemplo* (example). Crucially, the usual Q'eqchi' word that this Spanish word replaces, insofar as it is understood to have a relatively equivalent, or similar enough, Saussurean value or Fregean sense, is *na'leb'*, a nominalization of the verb *na'ok* (*to know*; including knowing *that a fact is true*, knowing *how to undertake an action*,

and knowing *someone*), using the instrumental suffix
-*leb'*, and hence literally "an instrument for knowing
(that, how, and who)."

Pues	a'an	jun	ejemplo	choq'	q-e		ajwi'	l-aa'o.
well	DEIC	one	example	for	E1P-DAT		also	DM-A1P

Well that [the story just told] is an example [or *na'leb'*] for us as well.

Li	k'a'ru	ta-Ø-qa-k'e,
DM	what	FUT-A3S-E1P-give

What we will give

li	k'a'ru	ta-Ø-qa-mayeja,
DM	what	FUT-A3S-E1P-offer

what we will offer

ta-Ø-qa-k'e	chi	anchal	li	qa-ch'ool.
FUT-A3S-E1P-give	PREP	all	DM	E1P-heart

we will give with all our heart.

Porque	wi	ink'a'	x-Ø-qa-k'e	chi	anchal	li	qa-ch'ool,
because	if	NEG	PERF-A3S-E1P-give	PREP	all	DM	E1P-heart

Because if we have not given with all our heart

pues	ink'a'	ajwi'	ti-Ø-x-k'ul	li	Dios
well	NEG	also	FUT-A3S-E1P-receive	DM	god

well then neither will God accept

k'a'ru	ta-Ø-qa-k'e	r-e.
what	FUT-A3S-E1P-give	E3S-DAT

what we give to him.

32. The Stories We Tell Are
(More or Less Equivalent to) Kula Shells

To return to the final paragraph of section 29, we can also talk about the value of this story per se. How many people have heard it, to what degree do they remember it, and how often do they retell it? How stable is its content (across such memories and retellings), how portable (or domain-general) are its precepts? How often, and to what degree, are the values portrayed internalized? How often, and to what degree, are such internalized values deployed to make decisions? See figure 31.

Note, then, that such stories are themselves somewhat like kula shells (themselves mediated by, and mediating of, the status, power, or renown of the people who give them; as well as the recognition of that power through others around them). And so we can examine their value in terms of their extension not just into space-time, following Munn, Karl Polanyi, and Malinowski, but also into deontic and epistemic modality; and hence not just into further reaches of the space-time-person manifold that constitutes *this* world, but also into the furthest reaches of *other* worlds.

For example, what kinds of worlds, for what kinds of people, could be governed by such stories' logics, should be governed by their logics, and are actually so governed? What worlds have they worked their way into? What worlds do they allow one to navigate through their workings? How wide or narrow have they spread? How deep or shallow do they sit? To what degree do people want to act under

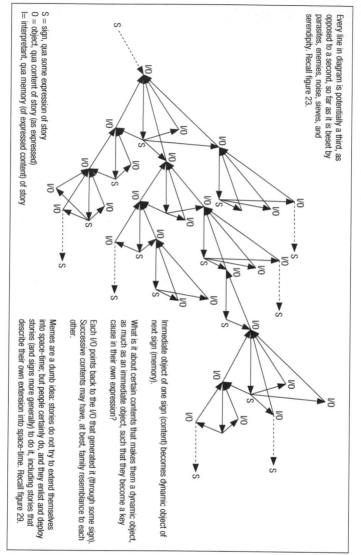

Every line in diagram is potentially a third, as opposed to a second, so far as it is beset by parasites, enemies, noise, sieves, and serendipity. Recall figure 23.

S = sign, qua some expression of story
O = object, qua content of story (as expressed)
I = interpretant, qua memory (of expressed content) of story

Immediate object of one sign (content) becomes dynamic object of next sign (memory).

What is it about certain contents that makes them a dynamic object, as much as an immediate object, such that they become a key cause in their own expression?

Each I/O points back to the I/O that generated it (through some sign). Successive contents may have, at best, family resemblance to each other.

Memes are a dumb idea: stories do not try to extend themselves into space-time, but people certainly do, and they enlist and deploy stories (and signs more generally) to do it, including stories that describe their own extension into space-time. Recall figure 29.

Figure 31. Extension of Story into Some Space-Time-Person Manifold
(through recursively reiterated semiotic processes)

such a description; to what degree do they feel they must; and to what degree do they actually do so?

Or, more pessimistically, to what degree have such stories, with their figured ideals, wormed their way into our own and others' psyches and schools, habits and institutions, imaginaries and infrastructures, words and worlds? How do such superstructures—not to mention the worlds they stand on, and the worlds suspended from them—stupefy us? To what end, with what effects, at whose behest, in whose interest, and to whose advantage?

33. Meta-ideals, Idols, and/or the Worthiness of Others' Worlds

Indeed, as interesting and informative as this story is, a certain kind of reader might wonder why, and indeed be disappointed because, it ends by idolizing an invisible man (which is not necessarily much better than golden chains or Lord Chajul), as opposed to opened eyes, enlightenment ideals, or truth value per se. (Recall from section 21, for example, the laudable, silly, insidious, and sinister ideals of SIL.) For just as there are standards by which we compare the relative value of different actions; there are metastandards by which we compare the relative value of different standards.

Phrased another way, there are *meta-ideals*—perhaps best called *idols*—by which we critique the relative value of others' ideals, the worthiness of others' worlds. Note, in particular, how many fetishes we've seen (here "<" = less than, in the sense of critiqued by):

The Golden Chain
    < Lord Chajul
        < God
            (< Ludwig Feuerbach)
                < Marx's Writings (on the fetish)
                    < Francis Bacon (that lover of truth value, historian of the enclosure movement, and theorist of knowledge and power, whose critique of the "Idols of the Theater" [or academy] was meant to apply to Aristotle's system, and would certainly apply to Marx's system, and probably to Saussure's and Peirce's systems as well).

To be sure, Bacon himself was unnaturally interested in metallurgy (in particular, the alchemy of precious metals like gold; just like Isaac Newton himself was unnaturally interested in the minting of money); so perhaps it really is a never-ending circle, each one critiquing the ones before it, and being critiqued in turn. ∎

Endnotes

1. See the wonderful collection of essays *Natural Histories of Discourse*, edited by Michael Silverstein and Greg Urban (Chicago: University of Chicago Press, 1996).

2. Miguel Sam Juárez et al., *Diccionario Q'eqchi'* (Antigua Guatemala: Proyecto Lingüístico Francisco Marroquín, 1997), s.v. "xiikil."

3. Frances Karttunen, *An Analytical Dictionary of Nahuatl* (Norman: University of Oklahoma Press, 1983), 326.

4. Laura Caso Barrera and Mario Aliphat Fernández, "Mejores son huertos de cacao y achiote que minas de oro y plata: Huertos especializados de Los Choles del Manche y de Los K'ekchi'es," *Latin American Antiquity* 23, no. 3 (2012), 291.

5. Robert Burkitt, "A Kekchí Will of the Sixteenth Century," *American Anthropologist*, n.s., 7, no. 2 (1905), 275, 288.

6. Ray Freeze, "A Petición of 1619 in K'ekchi' (Maya)," *Tlalocan* 8 (1980), 120.

7. William Sedat, *Nuevo Diccionario de Las Lenguas K'ekchi' y Española* (1955; repr., Chamelco, Alta Verapaz, Guatemala: SIL Publications, 1976), s.v. "-ajacual."

8. Ibid.

9. Mary Shaw, ed., *According to Our Ancestors: Folk Tales from Guatemala and Honduras* (Norman: University of Oklahoma Press, 1971).

10. Paul Kockelman, "From Status to Contract Revisited: Value, Temporality, Circulation, and Subjectivity," *Anthropological Theory* 7, no. 2 (2007), 153.

Conversations with Michael Cepek, Julia Elyachar, Asif Agha, Bill Maurer, Nick Enfield, Andrew Carruthers, John Lucy, and Michael Silverstein altered my approach to this topic. Fabian Muniesa, Stephen Twilley, Matthew Archer, Chris Hebdon, and Theodore Park offered very helpful suggestions. Many thanks to Matthew Engelke and Marshall Sahlins. For my mother, utmost among my inalienable possessions.

Also available from Prickly Paradigm Press:

continued

continued